FINANCE AND ACCOUNTING

A LANGUAGE OF ITS OWN

KEY DEFINITIONS IN

FINANCE AND ACCOUNTING

DAVID ROBINSON

FREDERICK MULLER LIMITED
LONDON

First published in Great Britain 1980
by Frederick Muller Limited, London, NW2 6LE

British Library Cataloguing in Publication Data
Robinson, David
Finance and accounting. – (Language of its own).
1. Accounting – Dictionaries
I. Title II. Series
657'.03 HF5021

ISBN 0–584–10546–6
ISBN 0–584–10556–8 Pbk

This book is set in 10/11½pt VIP Sabon by
D. P. Media Limited, Hitchin, Hertfordshire
Printed and bound in Great Britain by
Redwood Burn Limited
Trowbridge & Esher

Preface

Anyone who has dealt with an accountant, lawyer, banker or stockbroker will know that occasionally words crop up in ordinary conversation which seem to have a particular professional meaning. Many of these words have an everyday use as well. Take for example, the word 'asset'. We all use this word loosely to mean something which has value to us. But does it mean the same thing when used by an accountant?

The object of this book is to explain, in simple terms, what professionals are talking about when they use such words. Inevitably subtlety is lost in explaining things in a way which the non-specialist can readily understand. The definitions in this book must not, for this reason, be regarded as being exhaustive. They are not meant to 'teach' but to enable the reader to understand the essential meaning of the terms concerned.

The terms 'finance and accounting' cover an almost bewilderingly wide range of ideas and activities. Inevitably the personal experience and prejudices of the author play a large part in the selection process. I have aimed to provide simple explanations of the terms frequently encountered in bookkeeping and accounts. Added to this are definitions drawn from taxation, costing, banking and stockbroking. The whole is seasoned with other terms which may help to explain the difference, for example, between a Chartered and a Cost and Management Accountant or to summarise the job of various City institutions.

I hope you will find this an interesting and acceptable work of reference. If it helps you to achieve a better understanding of what the professionals are talking about, it will have more than repaid the time and effort involved in its writing.

D. F. Robinson

London 1980

A

Accepting house

A merchant bank which specialises in accepting responsibility for a bill of exchange (q.v.) in return for a commission. Although accepting a bill of exchange sounds complicated the principle involved is very simple. Imagine you agree to sell your neighbour a sack of potatoes for £5 and that he gives you a written promise to pay you that sum when you deliver it. The promise to pay is not worth much to you now unless you can persuade the corner shop to cash it for you. The shopkeeper will not do this until he is sure that your neighbour can pay and may even insist that you deliver the potatoes to him until he collects the £5. In essence the accepting house is the corner shop and the written promise to pay, the bill of exchange. Because it has an established name, and reputation for financial stability, it does not need to give you cash since its own promise to pay will be accepted as being as good as money. The accepting house in fact takes little risk since it usually trades only with buyers of integrity and also holds security for the debt until it is settled. There are at present sixteen merchant banks which are members of the Accepting Houses Committee in London.

Accounts payable

See Creditors.

Accounts receivable

See Debtors.

Accrual

Accrual is an idea which is fundamental to the presentation of accounts under the conventions used in most Western countries.

It is based on the principle that income or costs are allowed for when they are incurred and not when the money involved is either received or paid. It can be illustrated by the example of the domestic telephone bill. Suppose you draw up an account of how much do you earn and spend in the period from, say, January to March in a particular year. It may well be that you have made a lot of telephone calls but the bill from the Post Office has not been received because it is made up from December to April. From a *cash* point of view obviously you have paid out nothing on telephone calls in the period from January to March. On an *accrual* basis you have incurred costs on calls even though you have not had a bill. In calculating an income and expenditure account you should therefore show the amount accrued for the period. If you also prepare a balance sheet you would include the amount of the accrual in current liabilities (q.v.) as an amount which you expect to pay sometime in the future.

Acid test

An alternative name for the 'quick ratio' (q.v.).

Added Value

The amount by which a business increases the value of materials and services bought from other people by turning them into sales of their own finished products or services. A typical calculation of added value would be:

	£	£	
Sales of finished goods		250,000	
less Materials used	120,000		
Services provided by other people	40,000	160,000	
		90,000	= added value
less Wages bill	30,000		
Depreciation and Interest	20,000	50,000	
		£40,000	= profit

The added value total provides a measure of how well (or badly) the organisation is using its resources in terms of plant, money and people. Many companies reward employees by giving them a share of increases in added value. Such schemes give the individual a stake in the benefits obtained from both reducing costs and increasing profit margins. (*See also* Profit-Sharing Schemes.)

Advance Corporation Tax (A.C.T.)

Tax payable by companies on dividends which they pay to shareholders. The A.C.T. system was introduced in 1973 to simplify tax collection. What happens is that when the company pays the dividend it hands over to the Inland Revenue tax calculated at the basic Income Tax rate. The amount is calculated on the assumption that the actual dividend paid is the 'net' amount after tax. This is called 'grossing up'. It is done like this:

If the dividend paid is £100 and the basic tax rate is 30% then:

$$\text{gross amount} = £100 \times \frac{100}{70} = £143$$

The company pays £43 tax (£143 − £100). To prove the figures you can take 30% of £143 away from £143 to come back to £100.

The shareholder doesn't have to pay any more tax on the £100 dividend because it has already been paid by the company. The company can deduct the A.C.T. it pays on dividends from its other corporation tax liability.

Amortisation

The process of wiping out an amount of money over a period of time, literally, 'a mort' (to the death). Commonly amortisation refers to the writing off in accounts of an asset or debt. For example, a lease might be bought for a lump sum plus annual rental payments. If the lump sum was £50,000 and the life of the lease 21 years it would be normal practice to 'amortise' the cost by equal instalments of £2,381 (£50,000 divided by 21). This amount would be charged against the profits each year and the total value shown in the balance sheet reduced by the same sum. At the end of the lease the lump sum has thus been wiped out!

Amortisation is often used as a simple substitute for the word depreciation (q.v.) although there is technically a clear distinction between the two.

Annual General Meeting

An annual gathering of the directors and shareholders of every company, which is required to be held by law. The purpose of holding an annual general meeting is to make sure that certain legal requirements such as the presentation and approval of accounts, the re-election of directors and the appointment of auditors are dealt with on a regular basis. An A.G.M. is called by the Company Secretary and all shareholders are entitled to attend. The directors are generally prepared to answer reasonable questions about the company and its activities at the A.G.M. It is, for this reason, an important occasion since it is the only time of the year when the executives responsible for the running of the company are directly accountable to the people who put up the money – the shareholders.

Annual return

A statement made once a year by every company to the Register of Companies giving essential information about the company's activities and composition. The object of the annual return is to put on public record key information about a company's performance and financial standing. This enables lenders and organisations dealing with the company to judge how sound it is.

The law demands that an annual return will be sent in within forty-two days of the holding of an annual general meeting (q.v.). The return includes copies of accounts (except for unlimited liability companies), lists of shareholders, details of directors and lists of charges against the company's assets. Anyone can see copies of annual returns by paying a small fee at their local Company's Registration Office.

Annuity

An annual payment usually made to an individual for his or her life time. An annuity can be bought for a lump sum from, for example, an insurance company. Supposing you want to provide your elderly aunt with an income of £500 a year for the rest of her life. The insurance company will calculate how many years she is likely to live, based on statistical risks. They will then work out how much they are likely to pay out over the years. They will then calculate how much they would need to invest to cover this liability and leave them with a residual profit. Like all insurance, there is an element of gambling in this arrangement. If your old aunt lives a longer than average, life you will get very good value for your investment. If she gets run over by a bus the day after you bought the annuity, the insurance company has the best of the deal.

Appropriation account

A section in the profit and loss account of a company which shows how the profits earned, after tax has been deducted, are used to pay dividends and increase reserves in the balance sheet. Although this account is part of the profit and loss account, it is usually shown separately because it shows what happens to profit rather than how it is earned.

An example of how such an account appears might be:

	£'000	£'000
Profit for the year, after taxation		210
Take away:		
Ordinary dividends		
11p per share on 1,000,000 shares of £1	110	
Preference dividend		
7% on 500,000 shares of £1	35	145
	leaving	65
Then add:		
Balance of revenue reserves from last year		622
New balance of revenue reserves		687

Obviously if the company has made a loss in a year it may decide not to pay out dividends. However, the appropriation account provides the reader with a vital link between the profit and loss account and the balance sheet.

Articles of association

An elaborate name for a company's rule book. Every company must have 'Articles' and the Companies Acts suggest what they should contain. Essentially they record how the company should be run by the directors and what are the rights of shareholders. For example they will define what directors can and cannot decide without reference to the shareholders. Articles are rarely referred to in practice except when a dispute arises or a company is to be sold or to go 'public'. They usually contain important information for potential lenders to a company and to its customers. Changes in Articles have to be approved by 75% of ordinary shareholders.

Assessment

An estimate made by an Inspector of Taxes of the amount of tax a person or company should pay. Most taxes in the U.K. are based on the principle that the receiver (normally the Inland Revenue) calculates the liability and then asks the taxpayer for the money. The taxpayer always has the right to challenge the calculation he receives by showing in what way it is too high or, less commonly, too low. The assessment is the first step in this process. If the taxpayer agrees with the assessment he is then liable to pay up. If he does not agree, a process of consultation, negotiation and appeal starts.

If there is very little information for the Inland Revenue to go on when making an assessment, for example when a business starts up, this is recognised in the form of a 'provisional assessment'. The procedures and timetables for handling assessments are complicated and best left to the taxation specialist.

Asset

Something valuable that you either own or have the use of. In practice it is often something you have paid for, such as a building or machine which provides a source of income for the holder. If it does not wear out or become worthless within a year, the money spent on buying the asset is shown on the balance sheet rather than in the profit and loss account. Only an annual 'rent' for the use of the asset, called depreciation, is deducted from profit.

Land, buildings, machinery, motor cars etc., are called 'fixed' assets because you normally hold them from year to year. Stocks of goods you own and money owed to you or in the bank are called 'current' assets because they are normally expected to be turned into or settled in cash within an accounting year. These types of fixed and current assets are called, in total, 'tangible' assets because they can be, literally, 'touched'. Rights to a patent or a licence to make or sell a product are, in contrast, called 'intangible' assets.

Asset cover

The amount of security in the form of assets a borrower has available to cover the liability he takes on when raising a loan. Asset cover is obviously important to the lender since it is a measure of the funds which he might be able to obtain if the borrower could not repay the loan from his cash resources when the loan was due for repayment. There are two ways asset cover can be calculated. Using the simple method the net assets (q.v.) of the company are calculated then all the loans already outstanding are deducted as they would have to be repaid *before* the new loan. The 'rolled up' method is the same except that the new loan itself is included in making the calculation. The latter method is obviously more conservative and is the one normally used.

Associated company

A term used to describe the special relationship between two companies when one does not own the majority of the shares in the other but, nevertheless, has a position of influence over its activities. There are two types of associated company relationship defined in the Accounting Rules laid down by the Institute of Chartered Accountants. Firstly there is the situation in which the investing company is a partner in a joint venture. The companies concerned will be 'associated' whatever the level of shareholding involved. The second is where there is a long term investment of at least 20% by one company in the other and the investor can exercise significant influence over its management. This latter point can be quite difficult to decide in practice.

Why do companies need to recognise the special relationship of being associated? The simple answer is that the shareholders in a company making such an investment must be given the full financial picture in the annual accounts. If they only see that their company has taken an interest in another they may not realise the full implications in the longer term. By defining the other company as 'Associated' and giving full information about its finances they can better judge the soundness of the investment.

Auditor

An individual or firm who has the job of checking the accuracy of a set of accounts and giving a report on what he finds. Auditors are appointed by the shareholders of companies, not the directors, and address their reports to them. Every company is required by law to have an auditor who is 'approved' by the Department of Industry. Public sector bodies have similar requirements and the government itself has an Audit and Exchequer Branch. The bulk of company audits in the United Kingdom are carried out by either Chartered or Certified Accountants. An auditor must not be employed by the company or have any financial interest in it.

The job of auditor is in practice much wider and more complex than many people appreciate. Basically he is asked to express an opinion on whether the accounts show a 'true and fair' view of the company's finances. The words 'true and fair' often present the auditor with a problem. They are used in the Companies Act which, defines the auditors' responsibility, without any extra guidance on how they should be interpreted. The auditor must use his skill and judgement to make sure the truth and fairness of the accounts apply equally to the preparers and to the readers. This is often not as easy as it sounds. In addition he must examine and report on the compliance of the accounts with an increasingly wide range of standards laid down by the accounting bodies. One thing, however, remains unchanged, he is still the shareholders' 'watchdog' and not the 'bloodhound' unreasonably seeking out malpractice where it might not exist.

B

Back to back loans

An arrangement for borrowing money in one country based on lending an equivalent amount in another. Such loans give a company the opportunity to take advantage of more favourable borrowing terms abroad without transferring money to the country concerned. A back to back arrangement could involve, for example, a U.K. company depositing money with a bank in London. The bank will then arrange for its agent in New York to lend to the company's U.S. subsidiary an identical sum. If there is a cheaper rate of interest payable in New York the company obviously benefits. On the group accounts of companies with back to back loans the sums lent and borrowed are usually cancelled out. They are only referred to in the notes to the accounts.

Backlog depreciation

The amount which needs to be provided for additional depreciation in earlier years which would have been charged if an asset had been bought at its current cost rather than at its historical cost. This adjustment is only made in accounts which are adjusted to show the effects of inflation on the business. It is not used in accounts showing figures based on historical costs i.e., the actual costs originally spent.

The calculation of backlog depreciation can be illustrated by the following example. Suppose a piece of plant was bought in 1974 for £50,000 and depreciated annually at 10%. By 1979, five years' depreciation will have been charged, i.e. £25,000. If an equivalent asset would cost £90,000 in 1979, a new rate of £9,000 would be chargeable for depreciation each year. The inflation adjusted accounts for 1979/80 cannot correctly be charged with the whole of the difference in depreciation for the previous five years, namely: £9,000 – £5,000 × 5 = £20,000.

This 'backlog' must be written off directly against the new value of the asset in the balance sheet (£90,000).

Bad debt

A payment due to you which you cannot recover.

Where a company is concerned the amount is usually written off against profits in the accounts of the organisation to which the debt is owed in the year in which it proves irrecoverable. If it looks as though a debt might not be recovered, it can be 'reserved' in the accounts by writing it off against profits before it proves to be finally 'bad'. If some or all of the money due is collected, the reserve is reversed in the following accounting period.

Bad debt provision

An amount set aside in the accounts of an organisation to allow for the fact that some debts might not be recoverable. This is done by charging a sum as an expense in the profit and loss account. The amount is often calculated as a percentage of sales and the total amount provided can be 'topped up' or reduced year by year, as needed. The charge in the profit and loss account is reflected by an equal reduction in debtors in the balance sheet. A bad debt provision must relate to a specific debt and not to general amounts which might be recovered.

Balance sheet

A snapshot of the financial position of an organisation at a particular date. The total of which is owned (land and buildings, plant, cash, stocks, money due to be received etc.) is balanced by the capital invested by the owners plus what is owed (money due to others, overdrafts etc.). In simplified form a balance sheet looks like this:

What is owned – Assets

	£
Fixed Assets	
Land and Buildings	2,000
Machinery and Equipment	12,000
	14,000

	£	
	14,000	
Other Assets		
Money due from others	6,000	
Stocks	6,000	
Cash	2,000	
	£28,000	What is owned
		↓
Owners capital and what is owed – Liabilities		BALANCES
Capital		↑
1,000 shares of £1	1,000	
Previous profits retained	10,000	
	11,000	Investment plus What is owed
Liabilities		
Money owed to others	17,000	
	£28,000	

Balance sheets always follow these principles but vary considerably in presentation and content depending on the type of business to which they relate.

Bankrupt

Both the state of having insufficient funds to meet one's debts and the description of an individual who finds himself or herself in this condition. The term is loosely used to describe both people and companies who have gone 'broke'. In fact there are various stages and degrees of bankruptcy. Companies can still have prospects for survival even though technically bankrupt if their creditors agree to give them another chance. Equally a person made bankrupt can subsequently be 'discharged' by the court with the effect of giving them a fresh start.

The complications of bankruptcy law and procedure are a minefield for the uninitiated. Suffice it to say that bankruptcy is an extremely serious matter on which expert help from a lawyer or accountant should be sought without delay.

See also Undischarged bankrupt.

Bear

A person who expects the price of a share or commodity to fall and so sells what he does not own now to make a profit when he buys at a cheaper price later. Although it may sound strange it is perfectly possible to sell shares or commodities you have not got. The reason for this is that Stock Exchange deals are settled on the basis of a two week 'account'. This means that you can buy and sell as often as you like in that period and it is only reckoned up at the end of the period. Suppose the 'bear' expects a share worth £2 today to fall to, say, £1.50 in the next week, he can sell today at £2 but only has to have the shares to cover his sale at the end of the account. If he can but at £1.50 he makes a profit of 50p a share. If of course, the share goes up in price, he loses.

The term a 'bear market' is used to describe stock market conditions in which prices are generally falling. Like all generalisations there are considerable risks involved in assuming that a fall will apply to all shares in this situation. The reason is that there are always 'bargain hunters' for under-priced shares and 'bears' can easily be caught out if they are not careful.

Beneficial owner

The person or organisation which actually owns a property including shares in a company. Such ownership is 'beneficial' because the person concerned can buy or sell the property and receive any income from it without restriction. The term is important because it is quite common for beneficial owners to hide their identity by using 'nominees' who act for them. The nominee acts for the beneficial owner and must do as he is told by him. To make sure that, for example, the interests of directors in the shares of a company are not hidden by the use of nominees, the Companies Act makes sure that all such interests are disclosed in annual accounts.

Bill of Exchange

A document recording an order to pay a certain sum of money on a certain date. In commercial use a bill is prepared by a seller and sent to a buyer who 'accepts' it by signing it. It might say, effectively, 'I will pay you £10,000 in three months time'. When the seller gets the bill back he can either hold on to it or endorse it with his name and pass it on to someone else for cash. The next in line will, of course, pay less than the face value because he will have to wait for the bill to 'mature', maybe the full three months.

This is called 'discounting'. The discount amount depends on the financial strength of the buyer and current interest rates. If the buyer's credit is good the 'discount' will be a simple interest charge to repay the holder of the bill for having to wait to get his money. If the buyer's credit is not so good the discount will be higher to cover the risk of not being paid. A bill can be passed on from hand to hand being endorsed and discounted at each stage. When it is presented to the person owing the money the holder of the bill collects the full amount irrespective of what he paid for it. If the buyer cannot pay up the holder has a legal right to get his money in turn from each of those who have endorsed the bill.

This apparently complicated system works extraordinarily efficiently in practice. Many believe that the growth of the use of these 'negotiable instruments' made a major contribution to the commercial success of this country in the nineteenth century.

Bill of lading

An official receipt given by the master of a ship acknowledging responsibility for goods being carried. As soon as a bill of lading is given to the sender of the goods the shipping company takes responsibility for their safe delivery. This responsibility is not discharged until the person to whom the goods are being sent accepts them from the shipper at the port of delivery. Bills of lading are often used as security for borrowing money from banks as they provide formal evidence of ownership.

Bill of sale

A document given by someone borrowing money, giving the lender the right to claim and sell the property of the debtor if the debt is not repaid. Typically a pawnbroker's ticket is a bill of sale which gives the lender the right to sell the goods as an 'unredeemed pledge', if the loan is not repaid. Bills of sale are not commonly used for any other purpose.

Bonus issue

A way of giving the shareholders in a company more shares without them having to put more money into the company. This can only be done when the company has accumulated profits from previous years. For example a company might have:

	£
Ordinary shares	1,000
Past profits (reserves)	10,000

It could 'convert' the reserves into new shares and give each shareholder 10 new shares to add to each one already held. The position would then become:

	£
Ordinary shares	11,000
Past profits (reserves)	—

The shareholders effectively 'pay for' their own new shares and their interest in the company is unchanged. This is because the value of each share held is reduced pro rata to the extra ones issued. Bonus issues can be used to increase the number of shareholders by offering the opportunity for existing shareholders to sell off the new shares to which they become entitled to other individuals.

See also Scrip Issue.

Bought ledger

See Purchase Ledger.

Break even point

A point in time when a projected level of income exactly equals a projected level of costs. In the simplest possible example, if your income is £100 per month and your expenses £80 per month your 'break even point' is 8/10ths of the way through the month. If your expenses are £120 per month you never have a break even point at all!

The break even point is usually shown on a graph with the axes of time and money. A typical chart looks like this:

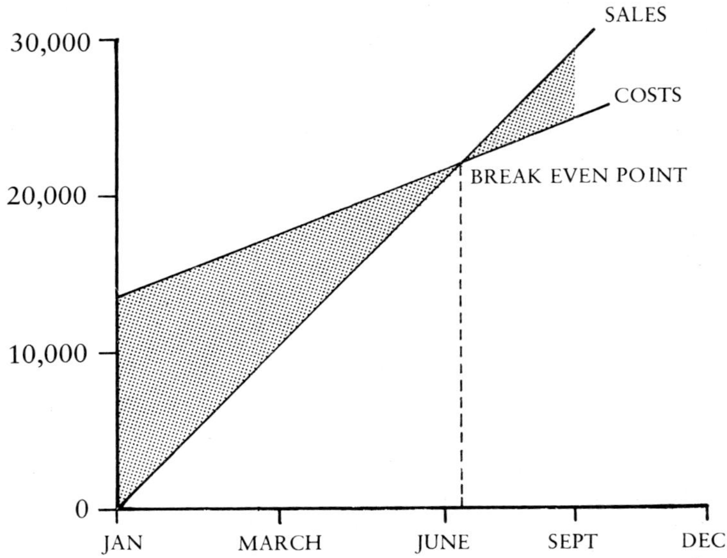

In this case the company 'breaks even' early in June. The gap between the lines up to then is loss and thereafter profit. The cost line does not start at the zero point because some money will be spent *whether or not* anything is sold. Break even analysis can become very complex and involve the use of computer techniques.

Bull

A person who expects the price of a share or a commodity to rise and so buys to make a profit on resale. Sometimes, the term a 'bull market' is used to describe a buoyant and confident stock market where there are more buyers than sellers of shares. To feel 'bullish' about a situation is to have confidence about the outcome. The opposite condition is to be a 'bear' (q.v.)

Nobody is certain where the term came from, but it is an eminently simple way to describe optimistic market conditions.

Budget

An estimate of the expected income and costs of future trading. A budget provides the manager with a practical guide to doing his job throughout the period the budget covers. It serves a number of purposes. Firstly, it involves giving very careful thought in its preparation to both sales and costs. This gives a considered framework to financial planning and, more particularly, highlights critical areas for attention. Secondly it lays down guidelines for controlling costs and finding revenue. Many managers can only spend 'up to their budget' and must get special permission to exceed it. Thirdly the comparison between budget and actual results pinpoints areas of variation which should stimulate management action.

Although the annual preparation of a budget is regarded by many as a time-consuming chore it represents a very important part of policy making. Without a budget to guide them, many companies have found themselves unable to cope with events which they should have foreseen.

C

Calendar variance

The calendar variance is used in management accounting reports. It shows the financial effect on the recovery of overheads of there being a different number of working days in two periods being compared. It is needed because overheads are often assumed to be recovered from production evenly through the year on a monthly basis. Since each month has a different number of working days the extent of over or under recovery in a month is analysed separately so that a common basis of comparison is used. The following simple example shows how it is calculated:

		Normal Month
A	Working days	21
B	Estimated monthly overhead recovery	£42,000
C	Recovery per day (B÷A)	£2,000

If a month being compared has only 14 working days the calendar variance will be calculated as:

Difference in number of days × daily rate
= 7 (21−14) × £2,000 (C, above)
= £14,000

This variance will be allowed for in the management accounts to avoid the danger that a false 'loss' of £14,000 on overhead recovery will appear to have been made.

Call

An amount asked for by a company as part payment for shares it has issued to a shareholder. A 'call' results from the fact that companies can issue shares for cash at less than their full face value. For example, a £1 share can be issued to shareholders, for 10p each. The outstanding 90p represents an unsettled liability of the shareholder which he is expected to pay up if the amount is 'called'. If the company finds it needs more cash it can call any part of the 90p per share it requires. The shareholder is obliged to meet the 'call' when it is due, or face serious consequences. The reason for this is that the issued capital of the company will be based on the full £1 per share value even though it is not fully paid up. A creditor of the company must be able to rely on the assumption that the balance of the amount outstanding will be paid in, if required, when it is 'called'.

The habit of issuing partly paid shares in the way described above has almost disappeared in recent years. As a result company 'calls' are becoming a rare if not endangered species. The government continues to do its best to keep the tradition alive by making a regular feature of the way it raises money through the issue of 'partly paid' gilt edged stock (q.v.).

Capital

Money invested in a business by both shareholders and lenders to enable it to operate with a view to profit. The idea of capital and return is fundamental to both economics and accounting. A balance sheet is designed to show how much capital was invested in a business at a particular date. The profit and loss account shows the return (profit and loss) made on that investment in a particular period in time.

According to many economists what constitutes 'capital' goes far beyond what is conventionally shown in the accounts. It has been agreed that it includes such intangibles as the loyalty and skill of the work force, the value of secret processes and the benefit of a brand name or share of a particular market. In the last analysis however, the measurement of success of an enterprise, at least in Western countries relies heavily on the financial value of capital. The component elements in this calculation are described elsewhere particularly under the headings 'balance sheet' and 'return on investment' (q.v.).

Capital allowance

A reduction in the amount of corporation tax payable by a

company based on the amount of money spent on capital items. The idea behind the granting of capital allowance is to give companies an incentive to invest in capital projects. The rates of allowances may change according to government policy but the principles of such a system have been established since the last war.

Under present regulations a company can claim 100% of what it spends on plant and machinery and scientific research against its tax bill for the year that the money is spent. It can also claim 50% of money spent on new industrial buildings in the first year and 4% each year thereafter.

Capitals Gains Tax (C.G.T.)

A tax on the profit made by an individual or organisation on the sale or other disposal of an asset. The term 'asset' is important in this context as profits on sales of goods or services in the normal course of business are subject to quite different Income and Corporation Tax rules. All assets are within the scope of C.G.T. unless specifically exempted. There is a long list which includes sales of private houses, motor cars and chattels worth £2,000 or less, and gifts to charities and other gifts worth less than a total of £100 in a year. The maximum rate of tax payable is 30% of the gain made. This is a complex tax and professional advice should always be sought when a liability to C.G.T. might arise.

Capital redemption reserve fund

An amount of money set aside by a company to buy back part of its capital when it is due. This type of fund is shown on the balance sheet and is made up of specific allocations year to year from profits made. It is shown as part of capital and reserves either on the accounts themselves or in a note.

The absence of a reserve fund does not mean that, for example, an outstanding loan will not be repaid. It could be that the company believes it can issue a loan note and repay the old debt with the new. It must nonetheless be true that the existence of such a fund is a considerable comfort to a lender who has any doubts about the ability of a company to pay up when the amount is due.

Capital reserve

Part of the accumulated capital of a business which is not paid out to shareholders by way of dividend. Before the Companies

Act 1967 it was compulsory for companies to distinguish between capital reserves and revenue reserves (q.v.) in their accounts. This distinction is no longer compulsory but is still followed by many companies. Capital reserves are created by what are, essentially, capital transactions. For example, if a company revalues its assets upward to reflect current market values the surplus is a capital rather than a revenue matter. By allocating such items to a capital reserve the company tells people that it would never intend paying those amounts to its shareholders as dividends. This shows the reader that the sums invested are *permanently* invested in the business and are not likely to fluctuate according to whims of the directors.

Capital Transfer Tax

A tax paid by an individual based on the value of cash, goods or property that he or she has given away during his or her lifetime and on death. C.T.T. was introduced in 1975 and, in part, replaced Estate Duty. The concept of the tax is much wider than the old Estate Duty covering, as it does, all disposals of capital and not just those occurring on death. It is a complex tax and, being so recently introduced, its application is being constantly clarified and modified by new case law. Its main principle is to tax all disposals subject to clearly defined exceptions including, for example:

a) property given by a husband to his wife or vice versa,
b) annual gifts to anyone of aggregate value of £2,000,
c) gifts to charities, and
d) gifts to pay for the school fees of a relative.

Many individuals take advice from accountants on how to reduce their liability to C.T.T. by tax planning. This, like many other branches of taxation, has become an area of considerable specialist skill.

Capitalisation issue

See Scrip Issue.

Cash flow statement

A document summarising the amounts of cash received and spent by an organisation during a period. It can cover either a period that has finished or one which has not yet started. In the latter case the statement is referred to as a 'forecast'. A forecast is usually compared with the actual results for the period at a later date to see what differences have occurred. Sometimes the forecast is 'rolled forward' by adding a new forecast period when one is finished. This is done like this: the January statement would include the forecast for December with a comparison with the actual result for that month plus monthly forecasts for January, February and March. The February statement would show the January forecast and actual result with new forecasts for February, March and April, and so on from month to month.

Cash flow statements are usually shown in the form:

	£
Cash from debtors	X
Less paid to creditors	X
Net trading cash flow	X
Less capital and other special payments	X
Net cash flow	X
Add Opening bank balance	X
Closing bank position	X

A good system of cash flow control through these statements is a fundamental part of the control of all businesses. Sadly it is a feature of many business collapses that this vital function has been neglected.

Certificate of origin

A document given by an authorised body to prove that goods were made in a particular country or place. These certificates are required by most countries before goods can be imported. The reasons are often as much political as commercial. Chambers of commerce, some government departments and trade associations are amongst those authorised to sign certificates of origin.

Certified Accountant

A member of the Association of Certified Accountants. The Association, which has some 21,000 members, emphasises a 'broad and practical financial training' for students most of whom qualify whilst working in industry or commerce. Certified Accountants are awarded the designatory letters A.C.C.A. and on admission to fellowship of the Association they take the letters F.C.C.A. Many top financial jobs in industry, commerce and the public sector are held by members of the Association.

Charter party

A contract between the owners of a ship or airplane and the hirers of it. A charter party contains details of the vessel, its owners and hirers, the journey proposed, hire rates, who is responsible for costs resulting from delays in the journey and so on. They are usually very detailed and formal documents. This is necessary because of the risks involved in transport by air and sea and the considerable costs which might result from accidents or negligence.

Chartered Accountant

A member of one of the three professional bodies of accountants which are regulated by Royal Charter. The three institutes are those for England and Wales, and one each for Scotland and Ireland. Several other Commonwealth Countries also have Institutes of Chartered Accountants although their constitutions are somewhat different from those in the United Kingdom.

A Chartered Accountant must train in the office of a practising Chartered Accountant for at least three years and pass stringent professional examinations. After qualification and admission to the Institute a member uses the designatory letters A.C.A. (C.A. in Scotland). After a period of five years a member is automatically elected a 'Fellow' of the Institute and may then use the letters F.C.A. after his name.

Chartered Company

The status of a few companies which owe their existence to a Royal Charter.

This was a form of setting up companies which was common until the middle of the nineteenth century. Well known examples are the East India Company and the Peninsular and Oriental

Steam Navigation Company (P. & O.). The rules governing such companies are basically the same as those set up under the Companies Acts except that they cannot change their Articles without the approval of the Privy Council.

Chartered Secretary

A member of the Institute of Chartered Secretaries and Administrators. This qualification shows that a member has both theoretical and practical training in company secretarial and administrative activities and a good understanding of financial and accounting techniques. Associates use the designatory letters A.C.I.S. after their names and Fellows, F.C.I.S. The Institute has about 44,000 members.

Chief Accountant

The person who makes sure that the books of a business are properly kept. This basic responsibility is often extended to include other aspects of financial management. In the last analysis, however, one thing that the Chief Accountant must do properly is to keep a complete and accurate set of books. Chief Accountants are almost always qualified in accountancy. The 'chief' part of the title suggests that they are in charge of other accountants and they often are. It is not uncommon, however, to find a Chief Accountant who is the sole bookkeeper, salaries and filing clerk employed by a firm! Such is the way with job titles that few qualified accountants would join really small companies for any lesser status.

C.I.F.

The abbreviation for 'carriage, insurance and freight', a term used to show that a supplier is responsible for costs of a product being sent abroad all the way to its destination. This term is contrasted with 'free on board' (q.v.) which limits the supplier's responsibility to delivering goods on to the vessel on which it will be shipped. C.I.F. contracts place the onus on the supplier to deliver the goods to a destination, usually a port, in good order before he can claim payment.

Close company

A company which is controlled by five or fewer participants or by its directors, to which special tax rules apply. The need for treating this type of company differently from others arose because the Exchequer was concerned that individuals could avoid high rates of personal tax by accumulating profits in companies which would pay tax at lower rates. By allowing profits to be held in companies the Exchequer obviously lost revenue. To overcome this problem a new category of close company was created purely for taxation purposes. The idea is that these companies can, in some circumstances, be treated for tax purposes as an extension of the individuals who own them. In this way income in the company can be treated as though it was the income of the participants.

Close companies have either to distribute up to 50% of their trading profits after tax or show a good reason for funds being retained in the business. The rules as to who are participants and how close company treatment affects individual firms are very complex. This is certainly an area in which professional advice should be sought.

Collateral

Extra security given to a lender in case the main security he holds should prove inadequate if he has to recover the debt. Quite often a guarantee is given as collateral by a third party. For example, a holding company might guarantee a bank overdraft for a subsidiary company which is also secured on the assets of the company. If the subsidiary company has a financial crisis the bank may 'call' the overdraft. If the company cannot pay up the bank will first look for recovery from the assets given as security. If these are not enough it will look to the holding company to make up the difference under the guarantee.

If the debt is not repaid the lender can choose which security he will go for to recover the money. If, for example, you borrow £10,000 you might give the lender the deeds of your house. Your brother might also give the lender a diamond tiara worth £15,000 as collateral. If you fail to repay the debt the lender can choose between selling the house or the tiara! Anyone who has tried to sell a house will know which the lender is likely to choose.

Collateral security can also mean that there are two or more items of security for the same debt. Rather than the collateral 'backing up' the main security, in this case all the items are equally available to the lender.

Commodity markets

The trading facilities which enable metals, raw materials and foodstuffs to be bought and sold in bulk in a freely competitive environment. Formal markets in some commodities are needed because both producers and users want to trade in large quantities quickly, simply and at a known price. Typical London commodity markets deal with gold, silver, tin, coffee, tea, rubber and cocoa. Some have a trading floor, rather like the Stock Exchange, where goods are bought and sold each day. Others have no physical marketplace but are made up of specialist brokers in touch with each other by telephone and telex, 'making the market'.

Typically a commodity market will cover both 'physicals' and 'futures'. Physicals are goods for immediate delivery and are often on board a ship either at or near the port where it will unload. Futures are contracts for future supplies which a user may need in three, six or twelve months' time. By buying in the futures market now, the user can fix the cost of the materials which will go into his product. The price of futures can depend on a mixture of factors such as inflation rates, crop size and so on. For this reason commodity markets often attract speculators who gamble on future rises and falls in commodity prices.

Company

See Limited by guarantee, Private company, Public company, Unlimited company.

Consistency

A principle of preparing accounts which proposes that items should be treated in the same way from year to year. It is an important concept because inconsistency would make a nonsense of the interpretation of accounts. For example, suppose that money spent on repairs to buildings was charged against income in the accounts of a company in a particular year. The profits would be reduced on what is clearly a perfectly sensible basis. Supposing, however, that the next year profits were not so good and also a lot of money was spent on building repairs. If the company decided to treat the expenditure as an asset rather than a cost, profits would be increased. This would be both inconsistent and misleading.

The auditor has the job of making sure that all such items are dealt with consistently between years. If they are not, he has a duty to say so in his report.

Company Secretary

An officer of a company who has specific legal responsibilities for keeping records of its formal business at board and shareholders' meetings. Every company must have a secretary formally appointed and such a person need not be a director. In private companies a sole director cannot also be the Company Secretary. One company can be appointed as Company Secretary to another.

The Company Secretary's formal duties include calling meetings, keeping minutes and the record books which the law demands that every company should maintain. In many cases he has many other executive responsibilities as well often centred on personnel and general administration. In some companies the job is also combined with that of Chief Accountant.

Consolidation

The act of combining the accounts of a number of companies which form part of a group. The purpose of a consolidation is to eliminate transactions between the companies within the group and to show the assets and liabilities which were bought when a subsidiary was acquired. For example, if Company A is a fellow subsidiary of Company B one might sell goods to the other. The second then sells the goods to the public. It would be wrong to show two lots of sales when showing the group position to shareholders. During the consolidation these inter-company sales will be eliminated. Similarly if a holding company bought a subsidiary for £1 million the purchase price might consist of:

	£'000	£'000
Fixed assets (land, machines etc.)		300
Current assets	600	
Less current liabilities	200	400
Goodwill		300
		1,000

In the consolidation these individual elements in the balance sheet are grouped together with similar items in the accounts of the parent company. Thus the fixed assets value (£300,000) will be added to the group total of fixed assets, current assets (£600,000) with similar group items, and so on.

The consolidation combines accounts for the parent company, subsidiaries and associated companies. All these terms are defined elsewhere.

Contingent liability

An amount of money an individual or company may have to pay out in the future but which cannot be said with absolute certainty to be a debt. A good example of a contingent liability is a guarantee given by a father to a bank for a loan made to his son to buy a motor car. If all goes well he will not have to make good a deficit on the son's bank account. On the other hand, he may be unlucky! If the father produced personal accounts he would have to show the guarantee as a contingent liability. In company terms contingent liabilities can be very significant items. The Companies Acts require companies to show the amount of such liabilities at least by way of a note on their accounts.

Contract costing

A system of keeping a separate record of the costs incurred and income earned on individual contracts carried out. The commonest and most obvious type of company likely to use contract costing is a contract builder. The outcome of each contract to build or repair a property needs to be calculated at the very least as a guide to estimating the cost of future work. Many other types of organisation have the same need. The principles of the system are simple. All costs and receipts directly concerned with the project are recorded in a separate account. The difference is the profit or loss on the job. In practice many complications arise because some costs, particularly overheads, have to be shared between projects and a fair basis must be found. Equally the work to be done may be varied and it becomes difficult to tell whether this is profitable or not. Other complications arise when a contract extends over several years and the amount of profit has to be calculated for inclusion in the accounts each year. Most of these problems have been resolved in practice and there are many good sources of information to help the accountant responsible for setting up a contract costing system.

Control account

A type of accounting record which is used to provide a check on the accuracy of another, more detailed, accounting record. The reason for needing control accounts is the vast amount of detail which many accounting records contain. Imagine, for example, the enormous number of individual sales that a large company makes each day. Each sale is recorded by an invoice and, in due course, each will be settled by a payment. The sales will be recorded in a sales ledger to which will also be posted the cash when it arrives. If someone fails to record an invoice or an item of cash it would be a formidable job to find the error. What is done is to record only the total sales figure and total cash amount each day, week or month in a control account. When the detailed sales ledger is checked the total of all individual items should agree with the total shown on the control account. If it does not, the difference can be isolated to a particular day or month and the error found much more easily than without a control account.

Control accounts are most often kept for purchases and sales ledgers but can be kept for any subsidiary records. The control accounts form part of the nominal ledger (q.v.).

Conversion period

The dates between which a convertible loan stock (q.v.) can be turned into some other form of stock or share. If a loan stock is described as 'convertible loan stock 1985/93' the conversion period will run from a given date in 1985 to another date in 1993. Both before and after those dates the holder of the loan has no right to convert. The conversion period is like a window which opens on one date and closes on another.

Ordinarily as the conversion period gets closer the loan stock gets more valuable if the stock or share into which it can be converted has a higher value. Suppose, for example, that you own £100 of loan stock which can be converted in 1985 to 100 £1 ordinary shares in a company. If each ordinary share is worth 135p in 1984 your £100 of loan stock, if you could convert immediately, would be worth £135. As the conversion period draws closer the amount of this difference, the 'premium', will become clearer. It will be worth more if the shares are likely to increase in value and less if they are likely to fall in value. People are often willing to buy these 'rights' and gamble on whether they will go up or down in value.

Conversion premium

The extra money you have to pay to buy ordinary shares in a company by buying loan stock which can be converted into ordinary shares at some later date. The calculation is made like this. Suppose a convertible loan stock carries the right to 'convert' into ordinary shares in three years time. Each £100 of stock can be changed into twenty ordinary shares. Now the price of an ordinary share today might be £4 each if you bought them through your stockbroker. So you could buy twenty shares today for £80. However, the ordinary shares might be expected to be worth a lot more in three years time. For example, they might be worth £6 each and 20 shares £120. If you bought the loan stock for £100 that capital profit plus the interest you receive in the meantime would be a bargain. As a result the £100 loan stock can be sold for more than £100 today. Suppose the value of £100 today was £102. The conversion premium would be calculated by comparing the price for each ordinary share you are paying by buying the loan stock today and what you would pay if you bought the shares through your stockbroker. In this example the premium would be 27.5% (comparing £5.10 a share (£102÷20) and £4 a share).

Convertible loan stock

A type of loan raised by a company which gives the lender the right to turn his holding into shares in the company. The reason for a company offering this opportunity is to make the loan more attractive when it is issued and so obtain it at a lower interest rate.

Loans are usually raised on 'fixed terms'. This means that the lender is entitled to an agreed percentage of interest each year on the amount involved and repayment of the capital at a future date. The lender does not get anything 'extra' in terms of dividend or share in the prosperity of the company. A convertible loan stock, on the other hand, aims to give the lender both the security of lending on fixed terms and the chance to 'convert' into shares which have these extra benefits.

Convertible loan stock is usually issued on a basis which commits the company to exchange the loan for shares between two future dates. This period is referred to as the 'conversion period' (q.v.).

Corporation tax

A tax on companies based on the amount of profit they make. The amount to be paid is calculated annually, usually based on the figures shown in the accounts. The tax is normally payable nine months after the accounts' year ends.

The standard rate of corporation tax is fixed in the Budget in retrospect for each year to 31st March. Small companies are taxed at a lower rate. Marginal reliefs overcome the risk of a company which earns only slightly more profit than the top figure in the lower rate 'band' paying a lot more tax than it should.

The calculation of the corporation tax liability of a company is a complicated affair. This is because a number of factors such as previous losses, allowances for money spent on capital items purchased and investment income received are taken into account. For this reason it is often not possible to calculate how much tax a company will have to pay simply by looking at its profit and loss account.

Cost and management accountant

A member of the Institute of Cost and Management Accountants. The Institute's qualification places emphasis on costing and financial control techniques in both theory and practice.

Members are not admitted to the Institute until they have had three years practical experience either during training or after passing their examinations. Associates of the Institute use the designatory letters A.C.M.A. and fellows F.C.M.A. Up to 1975 this body was called the Institute of Cost and Works Accountants and members used the letters A.C.W.A. or F.C.W.A. after their name depending on their grade. The name was changed to reflect the wider range of interest and responsibilities of members. Total membership is now approximately 17,000.

Credit

There are several common uses of this term. One meaning is to describe an entry in an account book which records a debt due or a liability. Credit entries are usually shown on the right hand side of the record although this is becoming less common with the wider use of computerised methods. The total of credit entries in a double entry bookkeeping system should equal the total of the debit entries.

Banks use the term credit to mean items added to a customers account. This means that when you have money in the bank, that money is owed to you by the bank. Thus, from their point of view it is a debt due to you which they must repay. If your account is 'in credit' with a bank it means you have funds on which to draw. If a business has a credit balance with other organisations it means it owes them money.

Lastly credit is often used to mean delaying payment for something you buy. To get credit the supplier you are buying from must be satisfied that you will be able to pay later. By opening a credit account they are simply recording a debt due to them.

Creditor

Someone to whom money is owed. The total value of the amount owed by a business is usually 'creditors' on the balance sheet. If the person to whom you owe money has the right to take an item of your property and sell it if you fail to pay him, he is called a 'secured' creditor. If he has no such right he is an 'unsecured' creditor. If a business goes bankrupt some debts, such as wages, have to be paid first. Those entitled to these sums are called 'preferential creditors' since their claim on the money available is preferred over other, unsecured, creditors.

Current assets

Items of property which a company expects to turn into cash within a year. They are shown in a separate section on the balance sheet. They usually follow the 'fixed assets' which are more permanent items of property used to earn revenue. The common categories of current assets are:

Cash and bank balances
Debtors – money owed to the company for sales
Stocks – raw materials and finished goods
Work in progress – goods in the process of manufacture

These items are 'current' in the sense that they are constantly flowing through the business. The total amount of current assets less the total of current liabilities is an important measure of the solvency of a company. A 'strong' balance sheet would show a good excess of current assets over current liabilities.

Current Cost Accounting (C.C.A.)

A method of accounting which aims to show the effect of inflation on a business. One of several alternative systems, C.C.A. is designed to show the particular effects of reducing values of money by adjusting profits in two principal ways. Firstly, by increasing depreciation to the amount which would have to be provided if the asset concerned was valued at its current replacement cost. Secondly, by increasing the cost of materials consumed in the business to their current price levels. These two adjustments can be illustrated as follows:

Plant Item	£
Cost in 1974	50,000
Annual depreciation at 10%	5,000
Equivalent cost in 1979	90,000
Annual depreciation at 10%	9,000
Additional depreciation for C.C.A. (9,000−5,000) =	4,000

Cost of Materials		£
Purchases for the year		200,000
Increase in prices in the year = 15%		
Average increase (6 months) = 7½%		
Cost of materials adjustment		
200,000 × 7½%	=	15,000

Accounts produced on C.C.A. principles would, in the above example, include £9,000 for depreciation and £215,000 for material costs.

The Institute of Chartered Accountants adopted, in March 1980, a system of Current Cost Accounting which requires larger companies to show in a supplementary statement to the accounts the main effects of inflation on the figures.

The system incorporates more complicated adjustments intended to reflect the impact of inflation on working capital and on the capital of the business where significant amounts are borrowed on fixed terms. Extensive guidance notes on this subject are available from the Institute of Chartered Accountants.

Current liability

See Liability.

D

Day book

A daily record of commercial transactions entered as they occur. In the early days of accounting every thing that was bought, sold, received or spent was entered into a day book, willy nilly. The items were then sorted out and posted to the books. Nowadays transactions are pre-sorted so that all sales invoices will be entered into a sales day book, all purchases into a bought day book, and so on. These day books provide total information for recording in control accounts (q.v), and often analyses by type of product, geographical area and other factors. Day books maintained on mechanised systems are usually print-outs which bear little resemblance to the bound volumes of former years. Nonetheless their function as primary records of the dealings of a business with suppliers and customers remains unaltered.

Debenture

Technically a document which acknowledges a debt. More commonly the term is used to describe a loan raised on the security of a piece of property on terms which include giving the lender the right to sell the property if the borrower fails to keep up the payments due. Usually a debenture is given on land or buildings – a house mortgage is a simple example – but they are also given on other types of property. In companies debentures are included in the capital section of the balance sheet and the interest rate and repayment date are usually shown thus: 10% Debenture 1993 – £40,000, meaning that the annual interest would be £4,000.

Debit

An entry in a book of account which records a debt which

someone owes to you or something you owe. Debit entries are usually shown on the left hand side of the record although in these days of computerised accounting this convention is fast disappearing. Where double entry methods are used, as is almost universally the case, the total of debit entries is equal to the total of credit entries.

Banks use the word debit in the, apparently, reverse sense from normal accounting. A debit to a customer's account reduces the amount in that account and not, as might be supposed, adds to it. This treatment is used because the bank's books are, in effect, a 'mirror' of those maintained by the customer. So if your account is in 'debit' you have an overdraft and owe the bank money. As far as the bank is concerned your debt to them is an asset.

Debit note

A record of a debt which is payable to the person preparing it. All invoices are debit notes although that term is seldom used in practice. It is more common for a debit note to be issued by a supplier to record an adjustment to an account. Thus, for example, a manufacturer might raise a debit note on a customer for carriage charges separate from an invoice already submitted for the goods themselves. Debit notes are also used for internal adjustments between accounts within the ledgers in an accounting system.

Debt factoring

A service offered by a finance house to enable a business to have the benefit of the cash due from its customers before it is actually collected from them. The business sends its sales invoices to the finance house which immediately pays them an agreed percentage (usually between 70% and 90%) of the invoice value. The finance house then collects the cash from the customer and pays the business the balance when it has been received. The charge for this service includes a collection cost as well as interest on the value of the debt outstanding. It is a more expensive source of funds for a business than borrowing from a bank. However, many firms find the speed and convenience of the system worth the extra cost.

Debtor

Someone who owes money. On a balance sheet the total cash due from others is usually referred to simply as 'debtors'. This total is one of the assets of a business since it forms part of what is owned. A customer becomes a debtor when his order is completed and an invoice is sent to him.

Defalcation

The criminal act of stealing money through the manipulation of accounting records. The term is usually applied where the culprit has falsified or destroyed records to deceive either his management, the auditors or both. Many cases of defalcation involve elaborate schemes which require great skill and ingenuity to unravel. Increasingly they involve the improper use of computer systems through manipulation of programs or using 'dummy' names of staff or suppliers. The auditor's job is to be alert to the potential for defalcation and to design his tests of the systems accordingly.

Deferred liability

A debt due to someone else which has been put off to sometime in the future. This type of liability is shown separately from other liabilities in the balance sheet. This is important because the person reading a set of accounts often wants to assess how much money the company can immediately lay its hands on to pay its debts. If debts payable quickly were mixed up with those to be repaid a long time in the future this would be difficult. Deferred liabilities are normally shown separately on the balance sheet so that they are not assumed to be payable immediately. Very often a note in the accounts will explain exactly why and for how long the liability is deferred.

Deferred shares

A relatively uncommon class of shares in companies where the shareholder's right to a dividend is deferred either for a particular period or until all other shareholders have been given a stated return. As can be imagined deferred shares are not a popular form of security! They are uncommon for this very reason and are usually only issued when a company has severe problems of either raising capital or financing dividend payments. The 'bitter pill' of deferment is often sweetened by the possibility of conversion into full ordinary shares before a certain date. Sometimes deferred shares are called 'founders shares'. These often give the right to receive a high proportion of profits above a certain total level but none below.

Deferred tax

A possible future liability to corporation tax which is not immediately payable. The term only came into the accountant's vocabulary in the early 1970s. The reason for this was the introduction of two measures by the Government. One was stock relief (q.v.) which allowed businesses to reduce their current corporation tax bill by a sum based on the increase in the value of stocks held. This was done to compensate for the effects of inflation in the cost of holding stocks. The other was to allow businesses to reduce their tax bill by the whole amount spent on capital items in one year. This was done to encourage investment. In both cases the tax liability was deferred and not extinguished.

After the concept was introduced businesses started to show the deferred tax in their accounts as a type of deferred liability. Very soon many balance sheets showed that as much of the capital in a business was represented by deferred tax as by shareholders' funds. This was clearly unsatisfactory and in 1976 the Government started progressively to extinguish part of this future liability. They did this by guaranteeing that they would never ask for some of the tax which had been deferred.

The rules governing the calculation and treatment of deferred tax are extraordinarily complex and like many other taxation matters they are best left to the specialist.

Depreciation

An amount included in accounts to represent the cost of using an asset. The principle involved is simple but its application is often complex. Suppose a company buys a machine for £100,000 and it is expected to last for ten years after which it will be useless. Although the company must pay for the machine immediately it would not be fair to charge the income of the first year with the full £100,000. If that was done a large loss might result. In later years large profits would follow because there was no charge in the accounts for the use of the machine. What the accountant does is to classify the money spent as an 'asset' (q.v.) and to write off a part of the cost each year until the machine is worn out. In this case the charge might be £10,000 a year for each of the ten years. And so what would appear in the accounts would be:

	In the Profit and Loss Account	*In the Balance Sheet*
	£	£
Original purchase		100,000
End of year 1		
Depreciation	+ 10,000	− 10,000
Net Value		90,000
End of year 2		
Depreciation	+ 10,000	− 10,000
Net Value		80,000
and so on until:		
End of year 10		
Depreciation	+ 10,000	− 10,000
Net Value		NIL

This illustrates the simplest, 'straight line' method of providing depreciation. A common alternative is the reducing balance method (q.v.).

Direct debit

An instruction given to a bank to pay money directly from a bank account on a regular basis. This type of instruction is commonly given when recurring payments are involved and the customer does not want the bother of telling the bank each time a payment should be made. Typical examples are mortgage, insurance and subscription payments. The customer has the right to cancel or vary his instructions for direct debit payments at any time. Direct debit payments are also known as standing orders.

Director

An officer of a company who has the authority to make valid contracts on its behalf. At first sight this may appear a surprising definition. The title 'director' is often seen merely as a means of having higher stature and more pay. However, in law, the power of the director to commit the company to a contract puts him or her in quite a different position from other colleagues. In recognition of this special position of directors, Companies Acts for many years have included detailed rules on both their rights and responsibilities. These include rules for appointment, automatic retirement (by rotation), removal from office, remuneration and loans and personal liability. Anyone can be a director of a company except undischarged bankrupts (q.v.) who must get the permission of the court first. Generally directors are not personally liable for the debts of their company unless they have taken credit for the company when they know for certain that the company will not be able to pay the debt. Directors may also be personally liable to the company if they act beyond their authority.

A private company must have at least one director and a public company at least two. Directors are appointed by, and can be sacked by, the shareholders. Their powers are laid down in the articles (q.v.) and their names must be shown on notepaper, including their nationality if they are not British.

It is increasingly common for companies to appoint associate directors or to distinguish between 'executive' and 'non-executive' directors. The principle in law is to assume that a director is a director whatever extra label is given.

Discharged bankrupt

Someone who has been bankrupt but has been allowed by the court to make a fresh start. By discharging a bankrupt (q.v.) the financial 'slate' is wiped clean whether or not the person has paid off all the debts which were outstanding when he or she went bankrupt. The person can once again be a director of a company and take credit (such as a mortgage or hire purchase agreement). Inevitably the label 'bankrupt' carries a heavy penalty in terms of the financial freedom of an individual even after being discharged. It seems certain that, as more and more credit records are maintained centrally in massive computers, this penalty will become increasingly severe.

Discount

A sum by which a seller reduces the amount payable by a buyer. Three forms are commonly found. Trade discount is a reduced price allowed to a particular type of buyer (frequently when the buyer is a business rather than a private individual). Quantity discount is given to encourage the buyer to increase an order. The allowance is greater if a larger quantity is bought. Cash discount encourages the buyer to pay more quickly. The total amount payable is reduced, usually by a fixed percentage, if the bill is paid within a stated period.

Discounted cash flow (D.C.F.)

A method of calculating the value of a business project. It is based on the idea that money which you pay or receive in the future is worth less than money at today's value. The further into the future this event lies, the smaller its value today.

The discounted value of a project is calculated by comparing, for each future period, what you expect to receive with what you expect to pay. The difference (the net cash flow) is then multiplied by a factor based on the annual rate by which you expect the value of money to fall taken from readily available reference tables. A typical calculation would be:

	Cash Out	*Cash In*	*Net Cash Flow In/(Out)*	*Factor*	*D.C.F.*
	£	£	£		£
Period 1	20,000	5,000	(15,000)	× 0.87	(13,050)
Period 2	6,000	12,000	6,000	× 0.67	4,560
Period 3	7,000	20,000	13,000	× 0.66	8,580
					90

The discounted value of the cash flow (in the example £90) can be compared with the project investment (£20,000 at the start of period 1). If it shows a greater sum than your investment you will make a positive return on your money. If it is less, as it is here, the project is not worth while.

Discount house

An institution specialising in discounting bills of exchange (q.v.). This service to banks and the commercial community makes cash available more quickly than if bills of exchange are held until the date when they become payable.

Discount houses buy and sell government stocks. They also accept and make deposits with the clearing banks and the Bank of England. These activities even out the day-to-day flow of cash through the banking system. At a discount house money is 'bought' and 'sold' as a commodity. Margins on interest rates and discounts are often very small but the sums they apply to can be huge. Discount brokers still do the rounds of the banks each morning wearing top hats, a quaint covering for a very sophisticated function.

Dividend

A regular amount paid out of the profits of a company to its shareholders as a percentage of the face (or nominal) value of a share. The percentage varies from year to year for ordinary shares which carry no automatic right to dividend if there are not enough profits to make a payment. The percentage is fixed for 'preference' shares. Preference dividends have to be paid out of profits before ordinary dividends.

The company paying the dividend deducts Income Tax from the total due and pays the net amount to the shareholder.

Dividend cover

An indicator of the relationship between the dividend actually paid by a company and the total dividend which could be paid in a period. Dividend cover is shown as a figure such as 2.5 or 3.

This figure is calculated by taking earnings after tax and dividing by the dividend paid. Thus a company making £500,000 profits after tax has been deducted and paying a dividend of £125,000 to ordinary shareholders, has a dividend cover of 4 (£500,000 ÷ £125,000).

If some of the earnings arise overseas the calculation of dividend cover becomes more complicated. Paying out all earnings may increase the total tax liability. Hence there would be less to distribute.

Dividend cover measurement is primarily a tool of investment judgement since it shows the margin between earnings and dividends paid. This is an important matter for the investor who wants to get the maximum return on his shareholding.

Domicile

The country in which a person has, for tax purposes, his permanent home. It is a concept of general law and is not defined in the Tax Acts. However, some tax liabilities only occur where an individual's domicile can be shown to be in the United Kingdom. Usually a person acquires a domicile at birth, that of his father, and only changes it by a later choice of permanent home. The acid test of change of domicile is that of making a permanent home in another country. A long period of residence there is not enough on its own to show that such a change has taken place.

Double entry

A system of keeping accounting records in which every financial movement is recorded twice, once on the 'debit' side of the books and once on the 'credit' side. If this is done accurately the books will 'balance' because the total of debits will always equal the total of credits. This method is now in virtually universal use in the Western world and is the foundation stone of all developed accounting systems. Originally thought up by Florentine merchants in the thirteenth century, double entry gives a person a means of making sure that he or she has kept track of all dealings, at least in total.

An example of double entry is buying goods and paying for them. When the supplier's invoice is received the total value is credited to the supplier's account and an equal sum debited to purchases. These two entries balance each other out. However, the books show that we own the goods and also owe the supplier for them. When cash is paid to settle the invoice the cash amount is credited and the supplier's account debited. The supplier's account is thus reduced to zero. What the books show is that the cash has been spent and the goods bought. A simple principle but one with great influence over the design and use of accounting records.

Double taxation relief

Taxation relief given to traders operating in more than one country to protect them from paying tax twice on profits earned in one country and sent to the other. Double taxation agreements operate between specific countries and there is no overall international system. Under a typical agreement a U.K. tax payer will be protected from paying Corporation Tax in the United Kingdom if the profits have already been taxed overseas at a rate equal to or greater than the equivalent Corporation Tax rate. If the rate overseas is lower than the Corporation Tax rate only the difference will be payable in the U.K. This type of arrangement only applies to profits and earnings *remitted* to the United Kingdom in the form of dividend. They equally only apply to income and not to capital transactions, such as buying and selling property.

E

E.D.

The abbreviation for 'Exposure Draft', a document produced by accounting bodies to promote discussion on some matter of principle affecting accounting policy or practice. The use of E.D.s has increased in the last decade as accountants have become increasingly concerned with regulatory standards used in the preparation and use of accounts. The exposure period involved is usually from six months to a year and is intended to draw together comments from a wide spectrum of public and private opinion.

Efficiency variance

The financial effect on the financial results of a period of having produced items more or less efficiently than predicted. Essentially a tool of cost accounting, the efficiency variance measures the value of production efficiency in terms of contribution to profit. It is a particularly important measurement where processes are highly mechanised since plant inefficiency can result in severe loss of overhead recovery and profits. The following example shows how efficiency variances are calculated.

	Estimate	*More Efficient*	*Less Efficient*
Number of items	10,000	10,000	10,000
Production Cost per Hour	£5	£5	£5
Time taken to make one item	4 hours	3 hours	5 hours
Total cost	£(4 × 5 × 10,000) = £200,000	£(3 × 5 × 10,000) = £150,000	£(5 × 5 × 10,000) = £250,000

	Estimate	More Efficient	Less Efficient
Efficiency Variance per item	—	+ £5	− £5
Efficiency Variance in period	—	£50,000 more profit	£50,000 less profit

Efficiency variance should not be confused with volume variance (q.v.) which measures the effects on profits of making more or less than predicted in a period at a given level of efficiency, for example, by working longer hours.

Emergency code

The code used in the P.A.Y.E. system (q.v.) when the tax allowances to which a wage or salary earner may be entitled are unknown or uncertain. The emergency code gives the individual the minimum possible allowances and hence he or she pays the maximum tax on earnings through P.A.Y.E. whilst the code is in use. Its use protects the employer responsible for tax collection from any later claim from the Inland Revenue if too little Income Tax has been recovered. From most tax payers' point of view, the sooner the emergency code can be replace by a full code, based on actual allowances, the better.

Equalisation fund

An account shown on the balance sheet of an organisation created to record funds set aside to keep an investment at a constant value. Such a fund is commonly set up to compensate for changes in the value of a foreign currency when an investment has been made overseas. Obviously if the value of a foreign currency declines the *effective* value of an investment made in sterling will also decline. To compensate for this an equalisation fund may be set up to cover the potential loss which might be incurred if the investment was converted back into sterling. The value of the fund will change from year to year depending on whether exchange rate values go up or down.

Equity capital

The total amount of money invested in a business by its owners. 'Equity' in this case does not have anything to do with the legal principle of 'fairness' between two people. It is simply a term used to distinguish between ownership on the one hand and lending on the other. The equity owners are all those who stand to gain more out of a venture if it is wound up than they originally put in. Someone who lends money to it can only, finally, get back what is lent. The equity owner, by comparison, stands to get more (or less) depending on what the venture or company is worth. Equity capital is therefore 'risk' capital to be lost or increased in value. In accounting terms the equity capital of a company is usually the total of the ordinary share value, and any preference shares which have the right to share in a surplus, plus the total of past profits and reserves accumulated on the balance sheet. The term shareholders' funds is often used as an alternative to equity capital.

Exceptional item

A receipt or expense which is worthy of special note in a set of accounts because it is untypical of the usual activities of the organisation concerned. Suppose, for example, that a company fights a law suit with a supplier over defective materials and wins a settlement of a large amount, quite out of proportion to its normal discounts. Although the receipt has resulted directly from trading it would be misleading to deduct the sum involved from purchases or add it to sales. It would be shown as a separate, exceptional item on the accounts to enable the reader of the accounts to compare the true results of trading in one time period with another.

The line between what is an exceptional item and what is an extraordinary item (q.v.) is often a fine one. The treatment in the accounts is very much a matter for the judgement of the auditor in consultation with his client. Happily there is usually a note included in the accounts to help the lay reader to understand what is involved.

Excess depreciation

An extra charge made in the accounts of a company in addition to the normal allowance for the wear and tear on assets to allow for the cost of their replacement. This is not a common practice but is designed to compensate for the fact that it will cost more to replace an asset when it wears out than when it was originally bought. This method has been largely superseded by the use of current cost accounting (q.v.) systems of adjusting accounts for the effect of inflation.

Exchange control

A system of controls operated by a government to limit the purchase or sale of foreign currencies by nationals of the country concerned. In the United Kingdom exchange control regulations were introduced shortly after the Second World War and were finally removed on 24th October 1979. Their objective was to conserve the country's foreign exchange reserves by making it difficult for individuals and companies to make investments overseas or 'export' foreign currency for other purposes including foreign travel. In practice companies could make investments overseas but the procedures involved, administered by the Bank of England, were complicated and time consuming. As far as individuals were concerned foreign currency for investment overseas could only be 'bought' from a pool, held by banks, created by sales of assets overseas by other individuals. This involved what was commonly called the 'dollar premium' which reflected the balance between demand and supply of foreign currency. Whilst exchange control has been abandoned by the U.K. it is retained by a number of countries and anyone trading overseas must be aware of these regulations to ensure that profits or capital can be repatriated without difficulty.

Extraordinary item

A receipt or expense which is so far outside the normal trading of an organisation that it justifies being treated quite separately in the annual accounts. A good example of an extraordinary item is the profit a manufacturing company makes when it sells its premises, perhaps to move to a larger factory. The company is not in the business of buying and selling property and so it would be very misleading to include the profit as part of trading activities. Nonetheless the profit has been made and it must be shown somewhere. The accountant's answer is to show the item at the end of the profit and loss account and write an explanatory note for the benefit of readers of the accounts.

The dividing line between an extraordinary and an exceptional item (q.v.) can be very narrow. It is often a matter for careful thought and fine judgement for both the company and its auditors. The guiding principle is that the accounts as a whole show a 'true and fair' view of the company trading results and the balance sheet position at the end of the period. If the accounts will be more true and more fair by showing an item as an extraordinary then that is how it will be treated.

F

Fellow subsidiary

Two companies are fellow subsidiaries if the majority of shares in each of them are owned by the same parent company. It is important to note that if the majority of shares are held by the same *individual* the companies concerned are *not* fellow subsidiaries. The common owner must be a company and hence they are members of the same legal group. Fellow subsidiaries usually have a close working relationship linked through common directors or through a controlling Head Office. This does not necessarily apply if they are active in different fields but they always have common allegiance to one parent.

F.I.F.O.

The shorthand form of 'first in, first out' which describes a method of stock valuation. This method assumes that the goods drawn from stock are those that have been there the longest. This can best be illustrated by the following example. If identical items of stock were bought, at different prices, over a period:

Date	*Price*	*Number*	*Value*
	£		£
January	1	100	100
August	1.20	200	240
November	1.40	50	70
the cost of the total stock would be:			410

If 100 are used in December, the F.I.F.O. method assumes that the 100 items bought in January are used first at a cost of £100. The stock that is left will be valued at (£410−£100) = £310 or £1.24 for each unit (£310 ÷ 250). If, in this example, the items used were assumed to have come from the last two batches the cost for each item would obviously be higher. The value of the stock left would, on the other hand, be lower than if using the F.I.F.O. method. F.I.F.O. accounting therefore tends to make the product cost lower but the stock value higher than other methods.

In periods of high inflation profits can be seriously overstated as a result of using the F.I.F.O. method. This is because the cost of replacing the stock used will be much greater than the amount charged against profits.

Financial Controller

A person who looks after the finances of a business on behalf of the rest of the management. The duties of Financial Controllers vary a lot between companies. Commonly they look after routine accounting, management accounts and reporting and cash control. If the company employs a Treasurer (q.v.) the job of the Financial Controller will be limited to more routine work. In many firms the Financial Controller is the number two to the Financial Director with the main task of putting policies into operation.

Whether the job of a Financial Controller is more or less important than that of a Chief Accountant depends very much on the size of the company and how it interprets job titles. Suffice it to say that the average Financial Controller expects to be rather better paid than a Chief Accountant in similar sized companies.

Financial model

A simplified mathematical representation of how the finances of a business work. A model is made up of a series of equations. These show, for example, that if sales are £a then debts will be £b or that if purchases are £c then stocks will be £d. In total these equations form a structure which can be used to show how the business will react financially to different circumstances. Models are usually built to be run on a computer although this is not essential. The great advantage of having a model is that management can test the effects of different decisions or measure the consequence of some new external factor, such as the rate of inflation, without actually committing the organisation to a particular course of action. They are a powerful aid to the manager and a godsend for the hard-pressed accountant. The use of models in the U.K. has grown at a disappointing rate in recent years. Perhaps this is one cause of many companies being apparently caught off balance when the foreseeable actually happens.

Fixed asset

Something owned for the purpose of earning income, either directly or indirectly. Machines and pieces of equipment are examples of fixed assets which are used directly to produce income. Factories, company cars and delivery vans are less obviously concerned with earning income. Nonetheless, they are also fixed assets. All fixed assets have a 'life' of more than one accounting period. If they did not they would be classified in accounts as an item of expense. Fixed assets are always shown separately in balance sheets. They are reduced in value each year by a depreciation charge. This is the charge to the profit and loss account for the 'use' of the asset in the year. If a fixed asset, such as property, increases in value it may be revalued to a higher value in the accounts. Normally fixed assets are shown at the original cost less all the depreciation charges over the years. This amount is called 'net book value'. It is *not* intended to show what the asset is worth if it was resold.

Fixed cost

A cost which does not vary with the output of the business. A manufacturing company has to have certain facilities to be in business. It must have a factory, machines, shop-floor workers, offices, salesmen, cars and lorries and so on. All these cost money. If the factory does not produce anything for, say, a day, these costs are still incurred. They are, therefore, fixed, at least in the short run. Obviously they vary over a period of months and years, partly because of inflation and partly because the business grows or declines. However, all businesses have a core of fixed costs which, unless they shut down, and sell everything, will always be incurred.

Fixed costs can be calculated in any organisation. They are particularly useful when budgets are being worked out since they show the minimum income to be earned to avoid a loss. They are also used when selling prices are set. This is done by making sure that each product makes enough profit to recover an appropriate part of the fixed costs of the business. Deciding how much of the fixed cost to charge to each product often causes problems. There are no hard and fast rules about this and every case must be looked at on its own merits. Knowing how to allocate fixed costs fairly is one of the skills of the good Cost Accountant.

Flexible budgeting

A system which aims to help the manager to control costs when the level of production varies from that assumed when budgets are fixed. Suppose, for example, a maker of widgets plans to make 10,000 items in a particular year. When he sets his budgets he will estimate the amount of money he will have to spend to make that quantity. If, in practice, he only makes 5,000 widgets he should obviously spend less money. The questions is how much less? Flexible budgeting aims to measure how much costs should vary in these circumstances. It usually forms a part of regular reporting during the course of a trading period so that the manager can see not only the past effects of changed output but also what the effect for the whole period would be if past trends continued. In this way flexible budgets highlight areas in which the manager can or must take action. A very valuable management tool.

Flotation

The process of making the shares in a company available to the general public by obtaining a quotation on the Stock Exchange. Literally the company is 'floated' on the public market to enable investors to buy and sell shares as they will.

The process of flotation or 'going public' as it is often called is long and complicated. It can be achieved in a number of ways, including by offer for sale, and by placing, both of which are described in the book. The Stock Exchange watches over those activities with great care to make sure that the general public is not misled or misinformed. Remembering the scandals of the eighteenth and nineteenth centuries, not least of which was the 'South Sea Bubble', this cautious attitude seems fully justified as a way of ensuring confidence in the stock market.

F.O.B.

The abbreviated form of 'free on board', a term used to show that a supplier is responsible for the costs of a product being sent abroad only to the point of despatch on the vessel. For example, if a company sells a car to a foreign purchaser the terms may be 'F.O.B. London'. The supplier is responsible for paying the cost of getting the car to the docks, clearing any port charges and loading it on to the vessel. The customer is thereafter responsible for the cost of shipment, insurance and loading, import taxes and so on. Very often the supplier's invoice becomes due for payment when he can show a 'bill of lading' (q.v.) which proves delivery on to the vessel.

Forecast

A prediction of the expected financial outcome of future trading or the results of a venture. A forecast is the 'best estimate' of the result. Quite often forecasts are given in a range. For example the company forecasts that the year's profit will be between £7 million and £7.5 million. A forecast should not be confused with a budget (q.v.) which is more of a financial plan. Forecasts are, however, often shown alongside budgetary information, particularly when circumstances have changed a lot since the budget was drawn up. The forecasts included in published documents issued by public companies are very carefully examined by the Stock Exchange. Obviously an optimistic forecast could improve share prices and a pessimistic one reduce them. Like all other speculations about the future, forecasts are only as good as the judgement of the person making them. Many commercial decisions are based on forecasts which have little more substance than informed guesses about the future. Some argue that this is unscientific. Many would agree, however, that there is much about business which cannot be predicted, and that the ability to make a reliable forecast is a rare and valuable skill.

Fourth directive

A set of regulations imposed by the E.E.C. on member countries which are intended to bring the presentation of accounts on to a common basis in all the countries. The directive takes effect in 1981 and requires each country to adopt a standard form of profit and loss account, balance sheet and cash flow statement. Some latitude is allowed to reflect vital differences in custom and law but the intention is to eliminate these over a period of years.

In the long run it will be theoretically possible for a reader in one country to look at a set of accounts prepared in another and immediately recognise items by their position and description. The changes involved are relatively small for the United Kingdom. However, many other European countries have very different conventions which will have to be changed radically. The extent of this change is such that there has been continuing opposition from a number of countries. It is also true to say that, although the presentation may be the same, it cannot automatically be assumed that audit standards or approach are identical. The accounts reader will therefore continue to have a problem of interpretation of accounts despite their apparent similarity.

Fraudulent preference

A payment made by someone going bankrupt to give the recipient an advantage over others entitled to share in any money available. The term applies equally to companies or partnerships and individuals. The principle is quite easy to illustrate. Suppose Mr. Bloggs owes a total of £10,000 to local tradesmen including £500 to his next door neighbour and best friend Mr. Smith. If he hands over all the money he has in the world, £200, to Mr. Smith saying 'I'd rather you had it than that lot' the payment is a fraudulent preference. The Trustee in Bankruptcy (or liquidator in the case of a company) can demand the money back and share it equally among all the creditors. That way each gets 2p in the £ (£200 ÷ £10,000) instead of Mr. Smith getting 60p in the £ (£300 ÷ £500) and the rest nothing.

G

Gearing

The relationship between the amount of the permanent capital in a business in the form of ordinary shares and reserves and the total value of loans made to it. In simple terms, measuring the gearing of a company indicates how much it relies on other people's money compared with its own capital. If a company has a low gearing (for example, has more of its own capital in the business than it borrows), it is obviously less vulnerable than one which is highly geared (for example, borrowing four or five times as much as its own capital). The reason for this is that if profits fall sharply, or losses are made, the lenders can exert more pressure on the highly geared company.

There are no 'absolute' levels of good gearing since the right ratio depends very much on the industry concerned. Stockbrokers and investment analysts keep a close watch on gearing as an indicator of the health of a company in comparison with similar firms in the same industry. If a company's borrowings increase out of proportion to its competitors this is often taken as an indication of impending problems.

Gearing adjustment

An amount, included in accounts adjusted for the effects of inflation, showing the benefit which a company enjoys by being partly financed by borrowed money. The inflationary loss in purchasing power is borne by the lender during the period of the loan. This is because the pounds that he or she recovers at the end of the period will buy less than they did when it was first granted. The borrower has a corresponding advantage. This must be taken into account when calculating the earnings and net worth attributable to those who own the equity (q.v.) in the borrowing company. A conclusion that can simply be drawn from measuring the effects of inflation on a company is that the higher the rate of inflation, the more advantage there is in borrowing money at fixed rates over a long period.

Going concern

A basic concept of accounting that assumes that a business will continue to trade in the future. Its significance lies in the very considerable difference between the value of an enterprise if it carries on its operations and if it stops trading. If, for example, a company relies heavily on the financial support of its bankers, the 'going concern' concept is very important. If its auditors have doubts about the continued support of the bank, their commentary on the state of affairs of a company could be very much affected by the possibility that it might fail. On winding up, a great many debts become due, and assets are worth only what they will realise at auction. This can be very different from the apparent value of their continued use in the business.

Goodwill

The excess of the amount paid for something over the value shown in the books of the seller. It may well be that a company is worth much more than the figure shown on its balance sheet. The reason for this is that the balance sheet shows only the money used in the business and not what it is worth on the open market. In a way a balance sheet is like a quantity surveyor's list of the materials in a house. Houses, however, tend to be bought and sold on the assessment of an estate agent rather than a quantity surveyor. The estate agent is not concerned with what materials went into building the house but rather with what it will sell for in the market. Companies are sold on the same basis of what they will fetch and not what is shown on the balance sheet. This means there is a difference between the two values which is called 'goodwill'.

The balance sheet contains details of what things have cost to buy but not necessarily what they are worth if they are sold. For example, if a company pays £200,000 for the shares in another with net assets of £125,000, the goodwill will be £75,000. This is shown as a separate item with other assets in the balance sheet of the buying company.

H

Human asset accounting

A theoretical way of showing on a balance sheet of an organisation the value of the people employed in it. Theories of human asset accounting were first developed in the United States during the 1960s and a number of practical applications were found in companies. The basic concept was to show how the investment in people employed in a company affected its performance. In particular the systems suggested focused on the value of training and developing good people compared with the cost of outside recruitment following high staff turnover.

Although a great deal of academic effort has been expended on human asset accounting theories in the past decade, it has so far had little impact on business. It is generally agreed that balance sheets prepared in the conventional way do not include one of the most important assets in most organisations – the people who make the profit. The search for a practical system which is also acceptable to accountants continues.

Hyde guidelines

The guidelines for the adjustment of accounts for the effects of inflation developed in 1977 by a working party under the chairmanship of Mr Hyde after the rejection by the membership of the Institute of Chartered Accountants of any compulsory system of inflation accounting. The Hyde approach concentrated on simple adjustments to bring accounts into line with current costs in place of the more complex system proposed by the earlier Inflation Accounting Steering Committee in Exposure Draft 18. These adjustments relate to the cost of materials consumed, depreciation of assets and gearing (*see* Current Cost Accounting). The recommendations of the Hyde Committee were largely incorporated in the Statement of Standard Accounting Practice (Number 16) adopted by the Institute of Chartered Accountants in March 1980.

I

Impersonal ledgers

Records of transactions which do not directly involve the dealings of a business with either customers or suppliers. The ledgers to which this term is usually applied are the nominal or private ledgers. These records show, usually in a summarised form, the financial effects of all the activities of a business. These will include the value of its sales and purchases, the wages paid, the expenses incurred, the capital invested, assets and liabilities and profits earned. The impersonal ledgers represent the core of any double entry bookkeeping system and it is from these books that trial balances are extracted. Another function of such ledgers is to 'control' subsidiary ledgers including the personal ledgers (q.v.). The idea behind using impersonal ledgers is to provide a summary of all the financial affairs of an organisation in a manageable and controllable form. Whether or not this is achieved is a matter for some argument!

Imprest

An advance of a sum of money to a person which is regularly made up to the original sum as expenses are incurred. Most petty cash systems are based on the imprest principle. A petty cash 'float' of say £100 is provided and expenses are paid out of this. Once a week the bills paid are presented by the petty cashier and the float is made up again to £100. It is a sensible way both to control expenses and to make sure that there is enough cash available to meet normal needs.

Imputation system

The system of collecting Income Tax on dividends from the companies paying them rather than from the shareholder receiving them. The name derives from the fact that the tax payment is 'imputed' to the shareholders by way of a tax credit. The system, which was introduced in the United Kingdom in 1973, makes tax much easier to assess and collect. Its operation is more fully described under the entry for Advance Corporation Tax.

Income and expenditure account

A record of the income received and costs incurred of a period which takes into account all transactions whether or not they have been billed by or to the organisation concerned. There is an important difference between this type of statement and a receipts and payments account (q.v.). This is because it includes outstanding items which have not yet been settled in cash. Consequently it gives a much better picture of the results of the period. For example, if a scout group reports its results for a year in an income and expenditure form it might include the following items:

	£	£
Income		
Subscriptions and sales of equipment		220
Sale of waste paper (cash not yet received)		80
		300
Expenditure		
Rent of scout hut (paid)	35	
Purchase of tent (paid)	100	
Electricity (bill not yet paid)	60	
Capitation fees (bill not yet paid)	40	235
Surplus for the period		65

Another interesting point to note about this statement is that both revenue and capital items are included in it. This is a major distinction which makes it different from a profit and loss account (q.v.).

Income cover

A measure of the ability of a borrower to repay the interest due on a new loan out of existing profits. It is normally calculated by adding together the borrower's existing interest on loans and the interest which would be payable on the new loan and comparing this with total profits before interest and tax. If the total of interest is half the total profits the 'income cover' on the loan is two. Lenders use this yardstick to assess how vulnerable their interest repayments might be to fluctuations in profits. It is rarely the sole test used and an asset cover (q.v.) calculation is also almost invariably used as well. This means that the careful lender has at least two measures of the ability of the borrower to keep up the interest payments.

Income Tax

A means of raising funds for government by collecting a portion of the income of individuals.

The amount which an individual has to pay is 'assessed' by tax inspectors in various categories defined in Schedules to the Taxes Act 1970. These cover revenue from property, income from investments, income from carrying on a trade, income from employment and so on. Virtually every conceivable type of income is assessed in this way.

The system involves giving the individual a number of 'reliefs' from income tax when calculating the amount of income on which tax is payable. These include personal reliefs, mortgage interest and life assurance premiums, and the cost of maintaining an aged relative. The net amount assessed is then subject to an increasing percentage scale of tax. The vast bulk of income tax is collected by means of the P.A.Y.E. system (q.v.).

The workings of the Income Tax system are extremely complicated and much brainpower is employed in the Inland Revenue (responsible for collecting the tax) and in the accounting profession (who advise individual taxpayers) in unravelling its many knotty problems.

Indemnity insurance

Insurance cover taken out by an organisation to cover the cost of making good losses suffered by their clients or customers as a result of its actions. The most common example of indemnity insurance is the cover taken by professional advisers against negligence claims. In recent years it has become increasingly common for companies, particularly in the United States, to sue their advisers if they suffer losses as a result of bad advice. Claims have often involved tens of millions of dollars although it must be said that more fail than succeed. The cost of providing such cover has now become a significant part of the cost of providing professional services.

Inflation

An everyday term which has a special meaning to the accountant who is trying to present figures in a meaningful way. Inflation is the reducing value of money as a means of buying goods and services. Thus a widget-making machine which costs £10,000 this year may cost £11,000 next (an inflation rate of 10%). The problem for the accountant is to show how inflation affects the purchasing power of the company in terms of both the cost of replacing the assets which it owns and maintaining an adequate level of profit on the capital it uses. There has been a number of attempts to find a generally acceptable way to measure those effects. The problem has been to find systems which are acceptable in terms of economic theory and, at the same time, comprehensible to the layman. The argument has been further confused by the popular contention that, by reflecting inflation in accounts, inflation itself is encouraged. The United Kingdom accounting bodies have now devised procedures to deal with this and only time will tell how effective they are.

Insider dealing

Buying and selling shares quoted on a Stock Exchange with the advantage of 'inside' knowledge is still a controversial matter. Anyone who has information which puts him or her in a better position than other shareholders to know the future course of the price of the share concerned is likely to be an 'insider'. Thus, for example, the directors of a company who know what the profits for the year will be before the public does would be acting improperly if they dealt in the shares on the basis of that knowledge. Insider trading is rightly regarded as being against the ethics of good business practice although there are, at the moment, few legal sanctions against those who practise it.

Institute of Taxation

A professional body made up of specialists in taxation. The qualification for membership of this institute is gained by examination, and is commonly held by accountants who already have a more general professional qualification. It is highly regarded amongst those in this specialised field. Associates use the designatory letters A.T.I.I. and Fellows, F.T.I.I. The Institute has about 6,000 members.

Institution

A term used to describe a substantial organisation involved in banking, investment, investment management or brokerage. Institution or institutional investor are terms often used incorrectly to describe any organisation with an office in the City of London. Although the word cannot be precisely defined in the financial vocabulary it is most frequently used of pension funds, investment trusts, insurance companies, banks, merchant banks, stockbrokers, finance houses, building societies and the Bank of England.

The institutions play a major role in the financial affairs of the economy since a large part of the nation's wealth, in the form of personal savings, passes through their hands. Their attitudes and actions have a strong influence on the performance of the stock market and the price of individual shares.

However, they are almost always acting as agents for depositors or premium payers and not as principals in their own right. This means that their first duty is to be prudent in their decisions. Some argue that this makes their attitudes unadventurous and negative. However, the potential conflict of interest with their duty to their depositors if they took too many risks is clear.

Integrated accounts

Financial records in which management accounts form an integrated part of the whole system. This means, for example, that product costs or monthly accounts are produced from the same financial records which form the basis of the annual published accounts. Such systems are more reliable than those which are separate because information is based on a firm foundation. In theory all management reporting systems should be integrated with finance records but in practice it is often costly and time consuming to make them so. The reason for this is that extra records have to be set up in the books to summarise and control all the transactions going through the management accounts or costing records. In addition control over the values recorded for stock and work in progress must be much more precise if the system is to work properly. Sadly many companies fail to recognise the potential benefits of using integrated accounting systems and soldier on with inaccurate or misleading 'management' figures. This can lead to serious errors.

Interim dividend

A part-payment of dividend on a share usually made after six months of trading. The assumption behind interim dividends is that the ordinary shareholders ought not to have to wait for a year between each dividend pay-out. The company when telling its shareholders, and the public, how well it has done after six months makes a payment 'on account' of the full year's dividend. This practice has been adopted by the large majority of publicly quoted companies but only rarely by private companies. Some companies pay more than one 'interim' during each financial year but most are content with 'half time' and 'final' payments.

Inventory

See Stock.

Investment income

An amount of money received as dividends from companies, interest from banks, government securities, building societies and so on. Companies have to show separately in their accounts the amount of income received from quoted companies and other companies. The terms 'franked' and 'unfranked' investment income are also commonly used. Franked investment income is the value of dividends received from companies. The paying company 'franks' the dividend by paying tax on it (*see* Advance Corporation Tax). Unfranked investment income is that coming from other sources and on which tax has not been paid. This includes almost every sort of interest and dividends received from overseas companies. The distinction is important in relation to the company in working out its own tax liabilities. Otherwise it has no significance for the investor or reader of accounts.

Issuing house

A merchant bank or finance house which acts as the selling agent for the shares of a company offered to the public at large. The issuing house is responsible for preparing and signing the prospectus (q.v.) advertising the sale of shares. It must therefore supervise all aspects of the preparation of the prospectus and be completely satisfied that all it contains is prudent and accurate. It is a heavy responsibility, since the success of the issue is often influenced by the reputation of the issuing house. The charges involved are correspondingly high.

J

Job costing

A system of keeping a separate record of the costs incurred in carrying out a particular job. One of the simplest examples is that of the garage repairing your car. They obviously need a way of knowing how much to charge you for the repair they did to your car as distinct from all the others they did on the same day. This is done by keeping an account of the mechanics' time and the spare parts and materials used. The time is usually charged to you at a rate which includes the wages cost, overheads and profit to the garage proprietor. The materials are charged at a price which also includes an element of profit. The total of all this is what you pay (with or without complaint as the case may be!).

All job costing systems work on these lines although in manufacturing companies the hourly charge may relate to a machine rather than to a man. Job costs often do not include any profit element since the object is to find the cost of making an item rather than to fix its selling price.

Journal

A book used to record particular transactions between individual accounts in a double entry bookkeeping system. While 'journal' literally means 'a day book', the term is now usually applied to a record used less frequently. Its main use is to provide a permanent record, with a narrative, of unusual movements between accounts. Say, for example, the directors of a company decide to write off a debt due to a firm because they do not think it can be collected. This will be done through the journal so that a permanent record is available. The item might look like this:

	Debit £	*Credit* £
Scroggins Manufacturing Co Ltd	20,000	
Bad debts		20,000

Being debts due to company written off in accordance with board resolution number 127.

The journal is also used where transactions involve both impersonal and personal ledgers (as did the example above). It is normally kept by a senior person in the accounts department and is a key record in the preparation and audit of accounts.

Journal voucher

A document recording movements between accounts in a double entry bookkeeping system. In essence a journal voucher is equivalent to one item in a company's journal. Vouchers are often used because a movement comes up regularly so it is simpler to pre-print vouchers than record them after each time. They also have the advantage that more information can be recorded on them than in a conventional record.

L

Labour rate variance

The financial effect on the profit and loss in a period of paying more or less per hour for the labour used in production. This variance is a type of price variance (q.v.) applied specifically to the hourly rate paid to employees working in production. It is used in management accounts and costing systems. It is a particularly important measure in those businesses in which prices are fixed in advance and labour costs represent a significant part of costs. For example, a maker of dresses might set his prices for the next season on the basis of present hourly rates of pay to cutters, machinists and so on plus 10%. If a national wage award results in his having to pay 20% higher wages instead of 10%, the effect on profits could be very great. The following simple example shows how labour rate variances are calculated:

		Estimate	*Actual*
A	Number of items	10,000	10,000
B	Production hours per item	4	4
C	Hourly wage-rate	£1.50	£1.75
D	Production cost per item (B × C)	£6.00	£7.00
E	Labour Rate Variance per item	—	(£7−£6) = £1
F	Labour Rate Variance in period (A × E)	—	£10,000 less profit

Letter of credit

A document given by a bank to a customer allowing him to draw up to a certain sum at another branch or an agent's office overseas. Letters of credit form a vital part of many international transactions. If, for example, a German company decides to buy goods in England, the English supplier may ask for a letter of credit from the customer's bank. This document will enable the supplier to be paid directly by a local bank part or all of the amount of sale when certain conditions are satisfied. It could be that the payment becomes due when the goods have arrived in Germany and have been accepted by the customer. It may be when they are delivered to the docks. In any event the letter of credit will state the maximum to be paid and the conditions which must be fulfilled before the supplier can make a claim. A general letter of credit can be withdrawn by the supplier but an irrevocable letter of credit cannot. If trading companies have not done business together before and a lot of money is involved it is common for an irrevocable letter of credit to be sought by the supplier. If goods are to be sent by ship, a documentary letter of credit is often used. The right to draw cash against the letter usually arises when goods are loaded and documents to prove this can be shown to the bank.

Liability

Something which is owed to someone else. A balance sheet shows both assets and liabilities. Typical items included as liabilities are: creditors – amounts owed to suppliers; bank overdraft – money due to the bank; taxation – tax due to the Inland Revenue; dividends – payments proposed in the accounts but not yet made. All these items are due to be paid within a year and are called 'current' liabilities. If they are not due to be paid for longer than a year they may be called long term liabilities. If a loan is made to a company for a long period it is usually included in the 'capital employed' section of the balance sheet rather than with current liabilities. A liability may also be 'contingent' in some future event or 'deferred' by agreement with the creditor. These terms are explained elsewhere.

L.I.F.O.

The shorthand version of the term 'Last in, First Out' which describes a method of stock valuation. The L.I.F.O. method assumes that the goods taken from stock are those most recently purchased. This can be illustrated by supposing the items in stock were bought at different prices over a period:

Date	*Price*	*Number*	*Value*
			£
January	£1	100	100
August	£1.20	200	240
November	£1.40	50	70
The cost of the stock was thus			410

If 100 items are used in December they are assumed to be drawn from the *latest* purchases namely:

50 of the £1.40 batch
and 50 of the £1.20 batch
So production is charged with
50 × £140 + 50 × £1.20 = £130.

The stock that is left is worth £410 − £130 = £280 or £1.20 for each item.

The effect of using a L.I.F.O. basis is to charge more costs to production and to value stock at a lower figure than if the first item purchased had been drawn first. Many favour the L.I.F.O. stock valuation method since it ensures that profits reflect most recent purchase prices. However, in times of rapid inflation the value of stocks can be seriously understated since the stocks which are held would cost much more to replace than is shown in the books.

Limited by guarantee

A type of company in which each member limits his liability for the debts of the company to the amount he or she has guaranteed to subscribe. This form of company is rarely used for businesses. It is common amongst charities and similar organisations. Although such companies may also issue shares they often do not do so with the result that a person's interest in such companies cannot be bought and sold in the conventional way.

Liquidation

The legal process which signals the death of a company. The term literally means turning all the assets and liabilities of the company into 'liquid' (i.e. cash) form and this is indeed what happens in practice. As a result the shareholders get back cash in return for the shares they own, if there are any proceeds left over after all debts have been settled.

In the vast majority of cases there are no proceeds for the shareholders and in a great many there are not even enough to pay all the creditors the full amount that they are owed. This is because most liquidations occur when companies can no longer pay their debts and, on sale, there are too few assets to cover liabilities. A minority of liquidations are undertaken voluntarily by the shareholders whilst the company concerned is still solvent. This might happen, for example, if the shareholders want to take their money out of a business to invest in something else.

If the company is insolvent, liquidation can be brought about by an unpaid creditor. The creditor must show the court that the company cannot pay its debts. If this is proved, a liquidator, usually an accountant, is appointed who 'winds up' the business as quickly and cheaply as possible and pays out what he collects to creditors. The liquidation rules are very complex and it is a specialist area of work for both accountants and lawyers.

Liquidity

A measure of the amount of cash a company can put its hands on quickly to settle its debts. The more liquid a company is, the more able it is to pay its debts and cope with unforeseen demands on its resources. Generally, therefore, a high level of liquidity is a good thing, although an investment trust, with the job of buying and holding shares for its members, might be criticised for having too much cash.

Various ratios are used to measure liquidity. They are all based on the principle of comparing how much cash the company could raise quickly with how much it might have to pay with equal speed. This information is obtained from the company's balance sheet and in particular from items included under the 'current asset' and 'current liability' headings. In common with many other ratios, measurements of liquidity have to be used with care. They must be based on a real understanding of the business involved and on the experience of similar companies in the same business. This type of analysis is commonly carried out by bankers (as one way of measuring the security for a loan) and by stockbrokers (as a way of measuring the strength of company in relation to its share price).

Listing agreement

A regulation imposed by the Stock Exchange designed to protect the interests of shareholders in companies with quoted shares. The word 'listing' refers to the list of stocks and shares which can be bought and sold on the open market through a stockbroker. The agreement is a set of rules contained in the Stock Exchange 'Yellow Book' (*Admission of Securities to Listing* published by the Stock Exchange, London). It requires that *proofs* of all circulars, minutes of meetings and so on should be approved by the Stock Exchange before being sent to stockholders. It contains a great deal of detail with which any quoted company, and its brokers, must be familiar if they are to avoid censure or even suspension by the Stock Exchange.

Loss

The sad financial consequence of unsuccessful trading. A loss is an excess of expenditure over income when costs have been adjusted for changes in the value of stock during the period concerned. Many companies and individual ventures suffer losses from time to time and still survive. Indeed in the early years of many new projects losses are to be expected. The tax laws of the United Kingdom recognise and are sympathetic towards loss making as long as the business is run 'with a view to profit'. Losses on trading can be 'carried forward' to reduce the tax payable on profits made in later years. Suppliers and lenders may be less helpful and unchecked losses precede most commercial failures.

M

Mainstream Corporation Tax

The final amount of Corporation Tax payable by a company after any Advance Corporation Tax (A.C.T.) (q.v.) has been deducted. Mainstream tax is therefore the amount which it is expected the company will have to pay on its profits. Inevitably the calculation is not as easy as it sounds since the amount of A.C.T. which can be deducted is subject to certain limits. Equally, if the company is a member of a group the Corporation Tax may be set off against losses in other group companies, a complicated matter.

Management accounts

Systems of reporting financial information which have, as their main purpose, the object of helping management to make better decisions. As a general term management accounts commonly include costing, monthly or quarterly accounts and budgetary control systems. They vary widely in type and value. They can be as simple as reports of orders in hand, cash available and outstanding debts. They can be highly complex including trends, variance analyses, statistics and so on. The most important factors in deciding what a business needs by way of management accounts are:

the type of business, e.g. a garage will need a job costing system (q.v.)

what is the key information that managers should have and when should it be produced

how much can management absorb and understand.

The last of these is often the least recognised. Managers are sometimes bombarded with too much information and as a result cannot see the wood for the trees. The secret lies in the famous advertisement for 'Erasmic' shaving soap: 'Not too little, not too much, but just right!'

Mandate

An instruction given to a bank to honour cheques when signed by specified individuals. Bank mandate forms contain details of the account concerned, specimens of authorised signatures and the date from which the arrangement is to run. It is common for companies and other commercial organisations to have two signatories on cheques. This acts as a security check to stop one individual making away with the firm's money. Alternatively a single signatory may have a limit on the amount to which one cheque can be made out. This information is shown on the mandate and if the bank pays a cheque for a higher sum they are liable for the difference if the signatory makes off with the funds.

Marginal cost

The cost of making an individual product 'on the margin' of existing or planned levels of production. The concept of there being such a product is important when fixing prices or deciding which of two products to make. If we suppose that a factory is geared to making 1,000 widgets a week it is reasonable to assume that we can calculate how much we need to sell them for to cover our costs and make a profit. This is simply a matter of adding up all our weekly costs, adding a margin for profit, and dividing by one thousand. If we ask, however, what it would cost to make 1,001 widgets and how much we could sell them for, the answer is not so straightforward. Obviously we should need one widget worth of materials and probably some more labour. Our machines would wear out a bit more quickly and we might spend a little more on heat and light. However we calculate it, the extra widget will not cost so much to make 'on the margin' as the 1,000 we normally make, nor do we need to sell it for so much to make the same rate of profit as on the others.

Knowing the marginal cost of production helps the businessman make better decisions about prices. If he has to choose between making widgets or nails on a machine, the one with lower marginal cost in relation to selling price will make more money. A useful tool for both the cost accountant and the business for which he works.

Merchant Bank

A bank which specialises in providing money and services to

industry and commerce. Merchant banks have their origins in the days of the rich merchants who financed sea voyages to trade with distant lands. The merchants provided the cash, and shared the risk with the sea captains. This provided the foundation of many family fortunes which were used to establish businesses which perpetuate the merchant adventurer spirit into the modern day.

Merchant banks vary enormously in size and range of services offered. They share in common, however, a willingness to invest in business enterprises and to provide cash in return for a share of profits made. The larger banks also provide advisory services, handle foreign currency dealings, finance imports and exports and will help companies who want to have their shares quoted in the Stock Market. One thing they do not normally do is offer a current account service to the private individual. This is the function of the High Street banks. Well known merchant banks originally founded by wealthy families include Rothschilds, Lazards, Barings and Warburgs.

Minority

Any shareholder or shareholders who hold individually or collectively less than 50% of the share capital of a company. Whilst all shareholders legally have the same rights, a minority cannot determine the policy of a company since they can be out-voted on major issues. The law protects minorities by not allowing companies to change their articles or reduce their capital without the consent of 75% of ordinary shareholders. This means that a 26% minority can block such changes if they disagree with them. In practice the influence of a minority depends on how the majority of the shares are held. In most public companies, for example, there is no single majority shareholder and so a minority with as little as 20% of the shares might be the most influential group. A minority in a subsidiary of a large group can also limit the freedom of action of the parent company. For example, a parent of a wholly-owned subsidiary can fix prices at which goods are sold by that company to other group companies at whatever level it likes. It is more difficult for the parent to do this if there is a minority involved. This is because the minority shareholders have no financial interest in the parent company or other, fellow subsidiaries. If the prices fixed were unrealistically low they would obviously be at a disadvantage when compared with the majority. Sometimes the interests of a minority are explicitly protected by a minority shareholders' agreement.

Mix variance

The financial effect on the recovery of overheads during a period of time of making different numbers of several products than predicted. A tool of costing analysis, this variance is useful where more than one product is made and each carries a different rate of overhead recovery (q.v.). For example, if a company makes nuclear submarines and egg boxes in the same factory it is likely that more overhead time and costs will be spent on the former than the latter. So each £1 of labour cost on a submarine might carry £5 of overhead whilst each 'egg box' £1 of labour carries 25p. At the end of a period, management needs to know whether they have recovered overheads by working with the same 'mix' between submarines and egg boxes that they predicted at the beginning. Too much time spent on egg boxes could, for example, mean less recovery and so less profit. The following simple example shows how mix variances are calculated:

		Estimate		*Actual*	
		Product A	Product B	Product A	Product B
A	Number of items produced	1,000	2,000	1,500	1,500
B	Labour cost per item	£1	£2	£1	£2
C	Overhead recovery	£3	£5	£3	£5
D	Total recovery per product (A × C)	(i) £3,000	(ii) £10,000	(i) £4,500	(ii) £7,500
E	Total recovery (D(i) + D(ii))	£13,000		£12,000	
F	Mix Variance (E Estimate – Actual)	—		= £1,000 less profit	

Money market

The collection of financial institutions whose main activities are to buy, sell, loan or deal in money. There is in London no market in the physical sense although most of the businesses which make it up are within the 'square mile' of the City. The Bank of England, the clearing banks and discount houses are very obvious money market institutions. Less obvious institutions are accepting houses, bill brokers, finance companies, merchant banks, bond dealers and stockbrokers.

Moratorium

An arrangement to postpone the payment of debts. Sometimes a company which is in financial difficulty can persuade its creditors to accept a moratorium. This could involve, for example, the creditors giving the company three months' grace before pressing for payment. Obviously the creditors must see a better prospect of being paid by waiting than by making the debtor bankrupt. This could be because the owners of a business are trying to sell it and the creditors may be paid by the new owner.

Mortgage

A right given to someone to claim a property if a loan made on its security is not repaid. Almost everyone is familiar with the domestic mortgage given by a building society or insurance company. The lender in this case makes a loan in return for holding the deeds of the property and getting a commitment from the borrower to repay capital and interest. If the borrower cannot keep up the payments the lender (the mortgagor) can claim the property and sell it to recover what is outstanding. So long as the borrower (the mortgagee) keeps up the repayments he can do what he likes with the property (except sell it) and the lender cannot interfere.

N

Net assets

The excess of the value of all the assets owned by an organisation over the money it owes at a particular date. The total of net assets is usually shown on the face of a balance sheet and is a very important indication of the value of the organisation concerned. The asset total is made up of both fixed assets (land, buildings, machinery and so on) and current assets (debts due to the organisation, stocks work in progress etc). From this total are deducted current liabilities which are essentially those debts owed by the organisation which have to be settled within a year. If the organisation has deferred liabilities, these should also be deducted. A typical calculation of net assets might look like this:

	£'000	£'000
Fixed assets		
Land and Buildings		210
Plant and Machinery		40
		250
Current assets		
Debtors		110
Work in Progress		60
		420
Less Current liabilities		
Creditors	225	
Bank overdraft	60	285
NET ASSETS		135

Nominal ledger

An accounting record containing the key financial information about capital, assets and liabilities and profit and loss. The ledger is made up of individual accounts which represent the 'impersonal' financial headings which appear in the statutory accounts. The entries in these accounts flow from the 'personal' ledgers (q.v.), the cash book, payroll and other subsidiary books. A system of double entry bookkeeping is not complete without this type of ledger. It is designed to summarise the overall financial affairs of the business in a way which makes it easy to measure what is owned, what is owed and what has been spent and received. A nominal ledger is rather like the sorting racks used in post offices. Each major account heading is like a 'pigeon hole' in the rack and each account entry a letter put in it. By selecting the pigeon hole you are interested in you can quickly check the total 'mail' it contains.

Nominee holding

Shares held by a person or an organisation on behalf of someone else. Nominee holdings regularly appear in lists of shareholders. They are 'nominal' holdings because the true or beneficial owner (q.v.) uses the name of the nominee to represent his interest. Banks and other financial institutional investors often use nominee companies to make investments on behalf of customers. It is easier to do this than to register each investor individually. Sometimes nominee holdings are used to attempt to disguise the identity of the ultimate beneficiary. However, the Companies Act gives companies the legal power to enquire into the identity of the ultimate holder. Both the Department of Trade and the Stock Exchange can use similar powers to investigate nominee holdings in special cases.

Non-voting shares

Shares in a company which enable the holder to participate in every way except voting. Commonly termed 'A' shares, this type of security is most often used to keep the control of the company in the hands of existing equity holders. By issuing non-voting shares a company can increase its capital base and not threaten the power of established shareholders. A non-voting shareholder is obviously a 'second class citizen' because he or she cannot influence decisions of company policy such as sales or purchases of subsidiaries. However, the successful and strong company can attract investors with this type of stock despite its disadvantages. The reason for this is that many people prefer to have a limited interest in the growth of a good company rather than none at all. Inevitably non-voting shares are worth less on the open market than equivalent shares with full voting rights.

O

Offer for sale

A means of selling the shares of a company to the public at large. An offer for sale usually takes the form of an advertisement containing the company's prospectus (q.v.). This form of sale can only be used if the company's shares are already traded on the Stock Exchange or if permission to trade on the Stock Exchange after the sale has already been obtained. Companies can use offers for sale to raise more capital. Equally a major shareholder can sell all or part of his stake in this way on a flotation (q.v.). The price at which the shares are offered is critical to the success of the sale. Fixing the price is left to the last possible moment before the offer is made public. The responsibility for this lies with the issuing house which also makes arrangements for any unsold shares to be bought by financial institutions.

Ordinarily resident

A term used to describe the status of an individual who, for tax purposes, is fully liable for all personal taxes in the U.K. To be ordinarily resident here the individual, of any nationality, must qualify as a resident (q.v.) for four consecutive years. The concept of ordinary residence is based on case law and the circumstances of each individual have to be considered before he or she can be said to fall into this category. Needless to say the great majority of those living and working in the U.K. are, for tax purposes, considered to be ordinarily resident here.

Ordinary share

A type of share in a company which gives the holder a right to participate in profits and capital growth, and usually in its policy and direction. Ordinary shares are the most common form in use. They usually have a face or 'nominal' value of between 10p and £1 each. The nominal value is normally the amount paid into the company for each share when they are first issued. Sometimes they are issued for less than the nominal value, the holder being obliged to pay the balance if the company asks for it at a later date.

The ordinary share has no guaranteed value after it is issued and the holder has no automatic right to dividends. This means that the ordinary shareholder takes a greater risk in investing in a company than someone investing in, say, preference shares which have fixed repayment terms and guaranteed dividends. Equally the ordinary shareholder expects to profit more from the success of the company.

The idea of sharing in profits and growth can be illustrated by a simple example. In the table below is a summary of the profits and net assets of a company at the end of each of two years:

		Year 1	*Year 2*
		£'000	£'000
	Trading Profit after Tax	50	300
Less	Preference Dividend	(50)	(50)
	and Ordinary Dividend	—	(40)
	Profit	—	210
	Net assets	1,000	1,210

In the first year all the profit is spent paying the preference dividend, which is fixed. If the preference capital is £100,000 the amount of net assets owned by the ordinary shareholders will be £900,000 (£1,000,000 less £100,000). In the second year there is enough profit to pay the ordinary shareholders a dividend and in addition their stake in the business has increased from £900,000 to £1,110,000 (£1,210,000–£100,000).

Overdraft

A short term arrangement by which a bank allows a customer to draw more money from his account than is actually in it at the time. Most people are familiar with the idea of being granted an overdraft up to a limit of a certain amount. After all it is one of the most common forms of borrowing. What is less commonly appreciated is that an overdraft is 'on call' which means that the bank can ask for its money at any time with, technically at least, no notice. If you cannot pay up the bank can pursue the debt in the courts and make you bankrupt. If they have security, such as the deeds of a property, they can force its sale. In practice, of course, banks rarely seek to recover their lending in this way. However, it is a sad fact that many companies live with a high overdraft level quite unaware of the potential effects of its withdrawal or forced reduction.

Overhead

A term used in management accounts and in costing systems. It is used to describe any expense involved in the running of a business apart from the costs of the material and labour directly spent on making a product or providing a service. For this reason overhead expenses are also often referred to as 'indirect' expenses.

The businessman or his accountant needs to know what the overhead expenses of his activities are for a number of reasons, not least to make sure that sales result in a profit after overheads have been paid. By classifying different types of overheads into groups they can also be controlled more effectively. For example, by analysing the costs of running a factory separately from those of selling the product and administering the business, responsibility can be delegated to different people who can be called to account for any overspending in their area. This idea proves the basis of all systems of budgetary control.

The very small business does not need to adopt any analytical approach to overhead costs because they are often under the direct control of one person. Nonetheless it is a fundamental principle of all trading that overhead costs are recovered in selling prices if a profit is to be made. This involves, in one way or another, the idea of including overhead recovery (q.v.) as part of the selling price of the product or service.

Overhead recovery

The process of getting back part of the expenses incurred in running a business in the price of each item sold. As explained elsewhere 'overhead' costs are those which are spent to keep the business running excluding the material and labour costs of making the product. The selling price of each item sold must recover these 'direct' costs, a part of the overheads and something extra if there is to be any chance of a profit being made. When prices are set the businessman has to estimate how much he has to add to the material and labour costs to achieve this.

Let us suppose that the material and labour costs of making a widget are £1 each and that the businessman expects to make and sell 10,000 in a year. If his overheads are expected to be £30,000 he might set his selling price in the following way:

		£
Material and labour cost for each widget		1
Overhead cost for each widget $\frac{£30,000}{10,000}$	=	3
Profit margin for each widget		1
Selling price		5

The business must make and sell 10,000 widgets at this price for the overheads to be recovered and the planned profit to be made.

If at the end of the year the company has made and sold only 5,000 widgets the management accounts might show:

		£	£
Sales of widgets (5,000 × £5)			25,000
Less			
Materials and labour (5,000 × £1)		5,000	
Overhead recovery (5,000 × £3)		15,000	20,000
			5,000
Less			
Overheads spent but *not* recovered (£30,000–£15,000)			15,000
	Loss		10,000

This example shows how important it is to link overhead recovery with a realistic view of the number of items to be sold.

P

Parent company

A company which owns a majority of shares in one or more companies and the majority of its own shares are not held by another company. The analogy with a family is apt since the 'children' (the subsidiary companies) must do as the parent directs. At least that is what happens between companies; whether or not that happens in families is another matter! The parent company relationship to its subsidiaries can be simply shown like this:

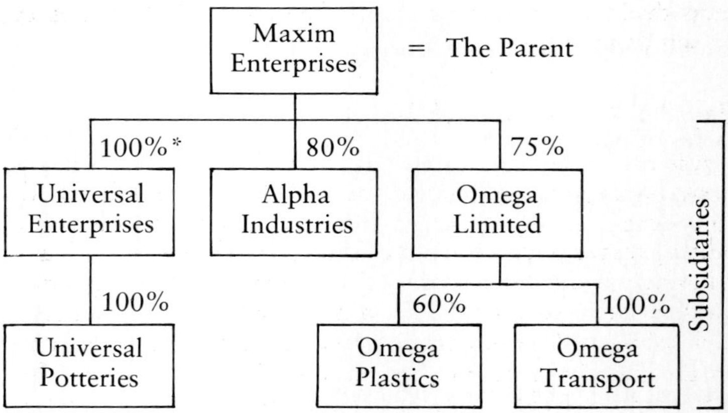

*All percentages show the proportion of shares held by the next superior company.

A chart like this can have as many tiers as you like. Each company is a subsidiary, apart from the 'parent'. In total they comprise what is usually called a Group.

Partnership

Any arrangement between two or more individuals or organisations which carries an undertaking to share the risks and rewards of a venture. The best known forms of partnerships are those of professional men who are often forbidden by the rules of their profession from taking limited liability. They share both the profits of their work and the risks of failure. In this latter respect any partnership requires that *each partner* bears not only his portion of a total liability but also any lack of ability of his partners to meet their shares too. This is known as 'joint and several' liability.

It is often thought that a partnership only exists if there is a written agreement saying how investment and profits will be shared. This is not so. If individuals or organisations act *as though* they are in partnership the law presumes that one exists. In the absence of a written agreement the financial arrangements between the partners will follow the rules laid down in the Partnership Act 1893. This includes the personal liability mentioned above. In the case of a total failure this could leave the individual partner with little more than his bed and the clothes he stands up in!

Pay As You Earn (P.A.Y.E.)

A system of collecting Income Tax from wage and salary earners based on the principle of deducting tax before the person is paid. Introduced in 1952, P.A.Y.E. revolutionised tax collection by putting responsibility for tax collection on the employer, thus relieving the Inland Revenue of an enormous administrative burden. The system works like this: the Inland Revenue issues tables showing for each week of the year what income tax is due on the cumulative earnings of an individual in the year. The amount due depends on the person's tax 'code' which reflects the total allowances to which the person was entitled in the previous year. Generally, the higher the code, the greater the allowances and the smaller the tax liability. The employer uses the tables to calculate the difference between the individual's total tax due in the week or month he is paying his wages or salary, with the total due last time a payment was made. This difference is deducted from the wages or salary payment and paid over to the Collector of Taxes once a month.

Each year, every employee is asked by the Inland Revenue to claim the allowances to which he believes he is entitled. If these are different from the previous year, the individual's code, and hence tax bill, changes. Codes are also changed during the year when, for example, someone gets married or has a child. Any over or under payment of tax due to coding changes is usually dealt with annually.

Payback

A simple method of testing whether an investment in a new project is worthwhile. It shows how quickly the profits from the venture will equal the capital to be invested in it. Suppose a new project will need an investment of £50,000. If the profits in the first three years are expected to be:

	Annual £	*Cumulative* £
Year 1	15,000	15,000
Year 2	25,000	40,000
Year 3	30,000	70,000

the payback period is between two and three years (since £50,000 is between £40,000 and £70,000). The exact payback period is the length of time it will take to recover the £50,000 assuming that the profits are made at an even rate each year. In this example the time will be:

Total for 2 years		40,000
Plus		
⅓ of the £30,000 in the third year	=	10,000
		£50,000

Equals 2 years + ⅓ year = 2 years 4 months

Perpetual inventory check

A system of regularly checking the accuracy of stock records used in a business. Most companies have a great deal of money invested in stocks. In order to keep track of what they hold they commonly use systems which record how many items are received and used. In theory these systems should show exactly the quantity of stock held at any particular time. In practice the records become inaccurate through human error and through pilferage and other loss.

The perpetual inventory checking system is based on the principle of counting every item of stock at least once a year and comparing the physical quantity held with the stock record. This is usually done by counting a certain number of items each day, week, or month. By the end of the year every item has been checked and the process can start again.

The differences revealed by this type of check can prove very helpful to management. In particular, weaknesses in paperwork or supervision can be pinpointed and remedial action taken.

Personal ledgers

Records of transactions between a business and its customers and suppliers. The word 'personal' in this context refers to the fact that the purchase or sale is between two identified organisations and not because individual people are involved. The personal ledgers in accounting systems are commonly the sales ledger and the bought or purchase ledger. The balances on these ledgers represent the total unsettled amounts either to be received or to be paid. They are usually controlled by means of total accounts which are used to ensure that they are accurate. Thus the organisation can keep track of both what it is owed and what it owes from month to month. The parallel of the personal ledgers in accounting systems is, not surprisingly, the impersonal ledgers (q.v.).

Petty cash

A fund for minor items of expense which are paid for in cash. Virtually every office or workshop has a petty cash box, often full of I.O.U.s! The 'little' expenses involved are best dealt with in cash and a 'float' is often maintained on an imprest (q.v.) system. Records are usually kept of petty cash movements but they are notoriously difficult to reconcile. The control account for petty cash is usually incorporated in the cash book because it is rarely worthwhile keeping separate accounts for such minor spending.

Placing

An arrangement by which shares in a company are 'placed' with institutional investors. A placing is arranged by a merchant bank or a stockbroker acting on behalf of a company the shares of which are traded on a Stock Exchange. Rather than offer shares for sale to the public in general a number of institutions, such as insurance companies, pension funds and investment trusts, are offered the shares privately to add to their holdings. When all the new shares being issued have been taken up in this way an advertisement is placed in the financial press recording that this has been done.

Pre-emption clause

A term written into the articles of a company (q.v.) whereby shares cannot be sold without first being offered to existing shareholders. This clause is exclusively found in companies whose shares are not quoted on the Stock Exchange. By reducing the saleability of shares it also reduces their value. However, shareholders are usually willing to accept a lower share value in return for protecting the company from an unwelcome takeover. This means that by exercising their right to 'first refusal' they can control who has a stake in the company. The wording of pre-emption clauses varies widely. Anyone intending to buy shares in a private company is well advised to read the clause with great care; at the very least he or she should know what problems might be met when they come to be sold.

Preference share

A part of the capital of a company which carries the right to be paid a fixed dividend each year. Preference share dividends must be paid before ordinary dividends. A preference share has a nominal or face value which is most commonly £1. It also has a fixed rate of dividend which forms part of the description of the shares, thus: on 9% preference shares of £1, 9p interest would be paid each year.

Some types of preference shares, called 'cumulative preference shares', have special rights. If the company does not make enough profit one year to pay the dividend, the unpaid amount is carried forward to the next year. When the company does have enough profits it must then pay all the arrears outstanding before paying dividends on ordinary shares.

Price/earnings ratio

The relationship between the total market value of a company's shares and the profits which it earns. The price/earnings ratio is a valuable means of comparing the performance of different companies. It is regularly shown in *The Financial Times* for the more active quoted shares. The reference to price is a bit misleading. What is compared in calculating the ratio is the current price of each share multiplied by the number of shares in the issue. This is the market value of the company. The earnings part is the profit of the company after deducting tax. A simple example of the ratio would be:

Number of shares × price = market value
1,000,000 shares @ 55p each = £550,000

Pre-tax profit − tax = earnings
£40,000 − £15,000 = £35,000
Price/earnings ratio is calculated £550,000 : £35,000 = 15.7:1

The ratio can be calculated for any company, although for private companies the market value is not so easy to define because shares cannot be bought and sold on the Stock Exchange.

Price variance

The financial effect on the results of a trading period of having to pay for goods or services at higher prices than you predicted. Essentially an analytical tool of costing, the price variance shows the manager the effects on the cost of a unit made and on the profits of inaccuracies in his estimate of the cost of purchases. This is important since prices are usually fixed before goods are made or services given and any error means more or less profit. This example shows simply how it works:

	Estimate	*More Expensive Materials*	*Cheaper Materials*
Number of items	10,000	10,000	10,000
Raw material cost	£30,000	£45,000	£25,000
Material cost per item	£3	£4.50	£2.50
Price variance per item	—	+ £1.50	− 50p
Price variance in period	—	10,000 × £1.50 = £15,000 less profit	10,000 × 50p = £5,000 more profit

Private company

A company which limits the number of members to fifty and restricts rights to buy and sell its shares. These restrictions are contained in the Articles of Association. There are three essential items: a restriction on shareholders' rights to sell shares, usually including giving existing shareholders first refusal; an undertaking not to offer shares or debentures to the public; and a restriction on the number of shareholders to not more than fifty (excluding employees and former employees).

The vast majority of companies in the United Kingdom are private companies. Those that do not comply with these rules are public companies. All companies are governed by the same legal requirements which are established in various Companies Acts. The most important Acts are those of 1948 and 1967. The particular advantage of a private company is that the shareholders can, to a large extent, protect themselves from an unwanted purchaser of their shares. This means that a family business can be kept in the family with a reduced risk of a takeover.

Process costing

A system of calculating the cost of making a single unit of production when the manufacturing plant works as a continuous process. Such a method would, for example, be used in an oil refinery or a factory making cornflakes. It is obviously impossible to measure directly the cost of making a tanker load of petrol or a packet of cornflakes. Process costing systems simply involve adding up all the costs and dividing them by the total of the output, to arrive at unit cost values.

Although it sounds simple it can be very complicated in practice because, for, example, in many factories a lot of different products are made by similar processes. In others valuable by-products are produced. In some, spoiled output can be recycled at various stages of production. The variations are numerous and complex. Luckily process costing is a well developed technique and a good cost accountant should have no difficulty in coping with the practical problems involved.

Profit

The welcome financial result of successful business operations. Strictly speaking a profit can only be calculated if all known income and revenues have been matched with all known costs, suitably adjusted for those costs applied to increasing the value of stocks. In practice the calculation of profit is a less than exact science and all statements of profit contain many approximations.

So long as the cardinal rules of consistency and prudence are observed when profit is calculated this does not really matter. Profit is one of the most important (and popular) measures of the success of an enterprise. In commercial terms it is less valuable an indicator of comparative performance than return on investment (q.v.). However it provides the basis for the calculation of tax liability and the payment of dividends. Profit is an important figure in the accounts of any organisation!

Profit and loss accounts

A financial statement which shows the result of trading operations in an accounting period. Profit and loss accounts are usually prepared for a twelve month period although this is not essential. Income is usually shown first and expenses are then deducted. Income is usually the value of sales excluding V.A.T. (q.v.) The raw materials and labour costs of making goods are then deducted, the difference being called the 'gross margin'. Other costs are then deducted to give the trading profit or loss as the case may be. A simplified statement would look like this:

	£'000	£'000
Sales		125
Less Purchases	37	
Factory wages	28	65
Gross margin		60
Staff salaries	18	
Rent and rates	7	
Other expenses	22	47
Trading profit		13

Profit-sharing schemes

Arrangements by which employees share in the fortunes of the companies for which they work. The term encompasses a whole host of possible alternatives. These range from the owner of a business giving each employee a year-end bonus based on results, to highly structured systems giving employees rights to buy shares at market price through specially created trusts. The existence of a scheme suggests rules and regulations governing the amount of profit attributable to employees and how it is to be shared out. Companies often use salary and length of service as key factors in working out how much each employee is to receive. Some use 'points' systems based on performance measurement and profit sharing may well be associated with job evaluation exercises. Under legislation introduced in the April 1978 Budget profit-sharing schemes can be used as a means of encouraging employees to buy shares in the companies for which they work. There is, however, an annual tax-free limit on such schemes. At the other end of the spectrum many small companies get into difficulty with poorly structured profit-sharing schemes for proprietor directors. These are frequently 'open ended', and as a result the money earned by one individual as a company grows becomes quite out of proportion to other people's earnings in the company. This can often lead to costly, and painful, results.

Promoter

A person who presents a new venture to those who are likely to invest in it. Very often a promoter has a personal stake in the enterprise and looks for backers who will trust his judgement and business sense. Theatrical promoters are well known for casting a wide net to find investors in new stage shows. Individual backers, known as 'angels', stand to lose all their stake if the show is a flop. If it turns out to be a box office success they not only make a profit but have the pleasure of being part of a successful venture. In the financial world new issues on the Stock Exchange, rather like debutantes, have 'promoters' who introduce the new shares to the market. Equally a new venture for which capital is needed may be handled by a merchant bank or stockbroker acting as its promoter.

Prospectus

A document prepared and published as an aid to the sale of a company or its shares. In simple terms a prospectus is the commercial equivalent of an estate agent's details of a property for sale. A prospectus must comply with strict legal requirements (laid down in the Prevention of Fraud Investors Act 1958). If a company, the shares of which are listed on the Stock Exchange, is involved there are extra rules to follow (laid down in the handbook, *The Admission of Securities to Listing*).

If a prospectus is used to help the sale of a company's shares it will usually contain information on its activities and history, an accountant's report on past results plus the directors' forecasts of future profits and the adequacy of cash flow. Very great care has to be taken in preparing prospectuses and company advisers including bankers, brokers, lawyers and accountants are usually involved. The penalties for issuing a false prospectus are severe. Not least is the damage done to the reputations of those involved in its publication.

Prudence

A concept underlying the preparation of accounts which states that future income should not be anticipated and that costs which may be incurred should be provided for. This concept is 'policed' by the auditor when he examines the contents of the accounts of an organisation. For example, suppose that a company wins a large contract to build a factory. It might be that the profit on the job will amount to £1 million spread over three years. The prudence concept determines that profits on the contract will only be taken into the accounts *as they are earned*. If the principle was not used the company could anticipate the £1 million profit in the first year and, perhaps, sell out on this basis. This would be unrealistic to say the least! The same principle applies to providing for costs which it can be shown with reasonable confidence will be incurred in the future.

Public company

Any company which is not a private company! This is a surprise to some people since a 'public company' is often assumed to be one with shares quoted on a Stock Exchange. Indeed getting a listing of shares on a Stock Exchange is usually referred to as 'going public'. However, if a company does *not* restrict its shareholders to fewer than 50, excluding employees and ex-employees, and does not limit the way in which shares can be bought and sold, it is 'public'. Such companies which are not 'listed' on a Stock Exchange are usually called 'public unquoted'. The most significant difference between private and public companies is the freedom with which shares can be transferred. A 'public' company is much more vulnerable to an unwelcome takeover because its shares can be freely bought through a stockbroker.

Purchase ledger

A record containing the accounts of transactions with individual suppliers. Usually organised alphabetically, each purchase ledger account shows both invoices received and cash paid. The purchase ledger has its origins in the spike of unpaid bills on the chief clerk's desk. Computerised systems have often reverted to this simple idea by dispensing with formal record keeping. Unpaid bills are kept 'open' until paid. If a creditor list is needed these items are simply totalled by the computer.

Q

Quick ratio

A measure of what would happen if a company quickly collected all the cash it was owed and settled all its debts. The 'ratio' uses the amount owed as 1 and the amount to be collected as the variable, thus – 1 : 1·2. If the ratio is less than 1 the company could not pay all its debts if they had to be settled immediately. A ratio larger than 1 means that there should be cash left over. Generally the higher the ratio the better. However, some traders rely on selling goods before they are paid for and commonly have ratios of less than 1. A good example of this would be a supermarket. The quick ratio or acid test (q.v.) is regularly used by bankers and other lenders when assessing the strength of their customers' accounts. It is of particular importance to them because they may have to claim their money back at short notice. If the ratio deteriorates it can be a warning of problems ahead.

Quoted share

A share in a company which can be bought and sold on a Stock Exchange as a result of its being 'listed' for public trading. This ability merely to buy or sell gives the shareholder a considerable practical benefit. It means that he can turn his shares into cash whenever he likes. The buying or selling price is solely dependent on the 'market'. If more people want to buy than sell, the price will rise, and vice versa.

The process of obtaining a 'listing' to enable shares to be quoted on a Stock Exchange is complex and costly. The company must show that it has a good record and that the shares will be attractive to potential investors. It must also be prepared to allow at least 35% of its total capital to be available to the public. Anything less than this would not provide an adequate 'market' for buyers and sellers.

R

Receipts and payments

A record of cash received and paid by an organisation during an accounting period. This type of statement is no more nor less than a summary of the cash book for the period. It does *not* take account of income which may have been earned but not yet received or costs incurred which have not been paid. This is an important distinction and a receipts and payments account should not be confused with statements which allow for those items (*see* Income and Expenditure Account). Receipts and payments accounts are often presented for clubs, associations and other small bodies. They can be misleading unless taken year to year. The reason for this is that if, for example, a bill received for rent or electricity has not been paid by the end of the period the result will look better than it actually is. A receipts and payments account cannot, for this reason, be linked with a full balance sheet which must include both amounts owing and owed.

Receiver

A person appointed by a lender, such as a banker, to collect money owed to him when a borrower fails to keep to the terms of an agreed arrangement, involving security specifically pledged to the lender. Typically a company wanting to borrow money will offer a lender the security of property or stock and debtors. In the first case the lender has a 'fixed' charge on the property and, if the borrower cannot keep up the repayments, will appoint a receiver to sell the property to repay the debt. In the latter case the lender has a 'floating charge' over part or all of the assets of the company. The receiver can either close down the business and collect debts and sell stocks or continue to trade as 'Receiver and Manager' until he has collected enough cash to repay the lender. The receiver, usually a practising accountant, has finished his job only when he has collected enough money to repay all the amounts owed to the lender plus his own expenses.

During his term of office he has very wide powers over the business and the normal powers of directors are suspended. Receivership often leads to either the sale of the business or its liquidation (q.v.).

Receiving order

A court order that puts the financial affairs of a bankrupt person in the hands of the Official Receiver. In effect it 'freezes' the individual's finances when it is issued to enable the Official Receiver, who is an officer of the court, to sort them out. It acts as a warning to the public that the bankrupt is no longer financially his own master. This means that if the bankrupt goes out and incurs a debt after the order has been made the Official Receiver can ignore it. Every receiving order is advertised in the *London Gazette* and everyone is presumed to have read it once it has been published.

In particular it stops any creditor from trying to recover the money or goods he claims from the bankrupt. This gives the Official Receiver the 'breathing space' needed to put the affairs of the bankrupt in order.

Reconciliation

The agreement of two sets of financial information obtained from different sources. Most commonly this term is used to describe the process of agreeing bank statements with a cash book. Usually done monthly, this reconciliation is needed to make sure that the two records are being kept accurately. Cheques which have been drawn but which have not been charged to the bank account appear in the cash book but not in the bank statement. In the same way payments made directly into the bank may be included in the bank statement, but not in the cash book. A bank reconciliation might look like this:

	£
Balance per bank statement at 1 July	10,000
Less cheques drawn but not presented	2,000
	8,000
Add cash received but not paid in to the Bank	1,500
Balance per Cash Book 1 July	£ 9,500

Accountants are familiar with the problem of trying, but failing, to reconcile two sets of financial information. In some cases a difference simply cannot be traced. In those cases a reconciliation statement at least helps to show how much the unexplained amount is.

Reconstruction

A reorganisation of a company or group of companies designed to improve its financial structure. A reconstruction is essentially a 'paper' reorganisation including shareholdings, reserves and the legal ownership of assets. They are often aimed at 'tidying up' groups in which shareholdings have become too complicated. For example, different minority shareholders may have small parcels of shares in different subsidiaries of a group. They might be offered, instead, shares in the holding company, so that all subsidiaries become wholly owned. The 'reconstruction' would involve issuing the right number of shares in the holding company in place of those given up.

Reconstruction may be needed for better tax management, to allow a subsidiary to be sold off or to prepare for the issue of shares on the Stock Exchange. Whatever the purpose, the techniques required to bring them off successfully are very specialised involving corporate finance, company law and taxation skills.

Redemption yield

The value today of the future income and capital gain to be made from holding a security until it is 'redeemed' at some future date, expressed as a percentage rate. This is a highly complicated subject and the yield calculation can be equally obscure. However, it involves, in essence, working out how much cash you would get year by year from holding a security that someone had promised to repay at full face value at a fixed future date and on which interest is paid in the meantime. For example, a government stock might be redeemable between 1998/05 and pay interest at 10%. You may be able to buy £100 of this stock today for, say, £84. The total cash you will receive between the time you buy and the earliest possible redemption date is then 'discounted' back to the present market value of £84. The redemption yield is the discounting rate needed to equate the values. Not a calculation for the layman but one which is regularly made, and published, by the financial press. It is used by professional investment managers to get the best value for money from their investments.

Reducing balance

A method of calculating annual depreciation charges based on a fixed percentage of the original cost of purchase of the item concerned. This method was popular in the United Kingdom until recent years but it has been progressively replaced by the straight line method (q.v.). The calculation is simple. If a car costs £10,000 and it is expected to last four years a fixed rate of 25% depreciation is charged each year. The depreciation charge and capital value will be:

	Depreciation charge £	*Capital value* £
When the car is bought		10,000
In the first year (25% of £10,000)	2,500	2,500
		7,500
In the second year (25% of £7,500)	1,875	1,875
		5,625
In the third year (25% of £5,625)	1,406	1,406
		4,219
In the fourth year (25% of £4,219)	1,054	1,054
At the end of four years the value left is:		3,165

Using this method there is (theoretically at least) always a value left (residual value) however long the system is used.

Register of charges

An official record kept by all companies showing debts which give the lender the right to claim against the property of the company if they are not repaid. The register of charges forms part of the 'statutory books' which must be kept under regulations laid down in the Companies Acts. The object of the register is to give any new lender the opportunity to check whether or not a piece of property offered as security is already spoken for. For example, a company might offer a lender a property worth £1 million as security for a loan of £500,000. If the property is already mortaged this fact will be shown in the register of charges.

Anyone can look at the register of charges of any company by going to the registered office of the company during normal working hours and paying a small fee. A copy of the contents of the register is included in the annual return which is sent to the Register of Companies by every company in the country. These records can also be inspected by the public.

Register of members

A list of shareholders which must be kept by all companies. The Companies Acts of 1948 and 1967 specify that this register must be kept at the company's registered office and be available for inspection during normal office hours. Large companies increasingly have their registers kept for them by bankers or professional firms using computer systems. This overcomes the problem of having to cope with occasional heavy workloads when, for example, dividends are paid, with limited staff available.

The register does not always show who actually owns the shares. The reason for this is the use of nominee holdings (q.v.) where, for example, a bank holds the shares on behalf of a customer. It is thus sometimes difficult for even the company itself to discover who is the person holding the shares.

Renounceable letter of allotment

An offer of new shares to a person that can be either turned down completely or transferred to someone else. If a company makes a new issue of, say, ordinary shares, it may have to offer those shares first to existing shareholders. If the idea behind the issue is to bring in new shareholders, renounceable letters of allotment may be used. The shareholder can reject (or 'renounce') the offer in the letter and so make those shares available to any other taker. Alternatively they can be 'renounced' in favour of some other specified person. This means that the company rules are complied with in giving the shareholder the first option to buy. At the same time shareholdings can be changed without a lengthy and costly legal process. Renounceable letters of allotment are often used in reorganising private groups of companies when shareholders agree to change the proportion of their interests.

Reserve accounting

A system of transferring unusual items in a set of accounts directly to the reserves shown on the balance sheet, rather than showing them in the profit and loss account. Whilst this form of accounting was common in the United Kingdom until recent years, it is now regarded as bad practice except for some privileged bodies such as banks and insurance companies. The reason for this is simple. If a company has the opportunity to disguise an exceptional loss on a venture by writing off the amount involved directly against reserves, the lay reader of accounts can be easily misled. The discipline of showing the item in the profit and loss account means that the item receives suitable prominence and, hopefully, comment from the directors responsible for it. The position of banks and insurance companies is rather different from the rest of the commercial community. They are allowed to use 'secret' or 'hidden' reserves to disguise their true performance to avoid the risk of a failure of confidence of depositors or investors.

Reserve fund

Cash or assets earmarked in a company's accounts to meet a specific debt. If, for example, a company has a debt to settle in five years time totalling £50,000. It may decide to set aside funds each year to meet the debt when it is due. This might be done by depositing cash with a bank (unlikely!), buying some sort of risk-free securities or taking out an endowment assurance policy. Obviously the interest earned on securities or a bank deposit helps to reduce the total amount which needs to be set aside. Few companies adopt this approach these days for the simple reason that money is better used circulating in the business than invested in low interest securities. Modern debentures (q.v.) also usually provide for a partial redemption over a number of years. This means that the company does not have to face the shock of a major debt repayment in one year and hence a reserve fund is not needed.

Resident

The status of an individual for tax purposes who is liable to pay Income Tax in the United Kingdom. Although the term resident is not defined in the Taxes Acts the concepts of 'residence' and 'ordinary residence' (q.v.) are established in case law. Broadly speaking a resident is someone who is in the U.K. for 183 days (not necessarily consecutive) in any one year, ignoring days of arrival and departure. If someone has a home in the U.K. he will be treated as a resident whether or not he visits this country, unless he is working full time overseas. Someone who comes to work in the U.K. for at least two years is usually treated as resident from the day of arrival to the day of departure. These general rules are, of course, subject to modification as case law clarifies the concept of residence. An accountant specialising in taxation matters should be able to advise on any individual case in the light of the particular circumstances.

Rest period

A technical term applied to convertible loans and not, as may at first appear, a reference to coffee breaks! It refers to the period of months or years between the time the loan is issued and the first date on which it can be 'converted' into some other form of security. The length of rest periods varies but they are rarely shorter than two years. Many run for five years or longer. The rest period can easily be calculated by looking at the description used in the accounts. If the loan is called 'convertible loan stock 1985/93' in the 1980 accounts the rest period is five years.

Revenue reserve

A total shown in the balance sheet of an organisation which represents profits of previous years which have not been paid out as dividends. Until the 1967 Companies Act came into force companies had to show revenue and capital reserves (q.v.) separately. Although this is not now required by law many companies still do so. From the point of view of the reader of a set of accounts a revenue reserve forms part of the total value of capital in use in the business. However, since a revenue reserve can be paid out as a dividend it is not permanent capital in the same way as equity or capital reserves.

Revolving credit

A special arrangement made with a bank to finance a series of transactions up to a fixed limit. Revolving credits are usually associated with financing imports.

The importer can effectively guarantee to the seller abroad that his bill will be settled. This is because the seller applies directly to the buyer's bank for the money due. So long as the importer carefully times the deposits he makes to his account and the bills to be settled out of it, he can use the total facility to finance an indefinite series of transactions. It is for this reason that the credit is said to 'revolve'. So long as the customer is financially sound it is good business for the bank too.

Rights issue

A way of raising new capital for a company by which existing shareholders can buy new shares more cheaply than the market price of the ones they already hold. If, for example, the quoted price of a share on the stock market is 100p the shareholders might be offered the 'right' to buy one new share for each one they already hold at a price of 90p. The shareholder does not have to buy the shares offered. If he decides not to take them up, his 'rights' are bought by an underwriter who, for a fee, guarantees to the company that all the shares will be sold. The underwriter will also pay the company 90p for each share he has to take up but will also charge a fee to the company for this service. All the proceeds add to the capital of the company. Rights issues are commonly used to raise money for new investment being planned by the company concerned.

Roll over relief

A relief granted by tax laws which postpones the payment of Capital Gains Tax (C.G.T. q.v.). It applies when the proceeds of the sale of an asset are reinvested in a new, similar asset. For example the sale of a warehouse by a company might result in a liability to pay C.G.T. on the excess of the sale price over the purchase price (if bought after 1965). If the company buys another commerical premises with the proceeds the 'gain' is rolled over until the new asset is eventually sold (or rolled over again). On the ultimate sale the total amount taxable picks up all the gains rolled over in the chain. The extent to which a capital gain has been rolled over is not usually apparent from the annual accounts because it forms a part of tax calculations which are not normally shown in detail.

Romalpa clause

A clause which can be included in the conditions of sale of goods whereby the seller reserves the right to reclaim the goods if they have not been paid for after a specified time. Although this form of 'reservation of title' has been available to suppliers for many years, it came to prominence in a major case in 1976 (Aluminium Industrie Vaasen B.V. *v* Romalpa). The suppliers in this case recovered stocks of materials held by their customer (Romalpa) after the latter company had gone bankrupt. If such a clause had not been included in the conditions of sale, the supplier could only have claimed as an unsecured creditor recovering, perhaps, only part of the money owed. As it was, the clause gave the supplier the right to seize the goods and, indeed, claim items that had been sold on by the customer and could still be traced. The effect of a Romalpa clause, as far as the customer is concerned, is to reduce the total value of his stocks and work in progress available as 'cover' for a loan. This is because a lender, for example a bank, will not lend money against assets which might be claimed by someone else in the event of a winding up.

Rule of 78

A method sometimes used by finance companies to spread their return on a loan over the period for which it is made. The problem the finance company has to solve is to divide a fixed monthly repayment between a sum to pay for interest and a sum to repay capital. As is commonly known more interest is paid during the early years of a mortgage than towards its finish. This is because the repayments must first cover the interest, and then what is over reduces the capital. Over a period the interest element reduces leaving a greater and greater amount to offset against capital.

The rule of 78 method is a way of calculating the interest part in a repayment. It is based on adding together the number of each week, month or year that a loan is going to last. It gets its name from the fact that a one year agreement with monthly payments will have, as a sum of the months, 78. This is calculated by adding 1+2+3 etc., up to 12. What the finance house does is to say that in the first month of a year's agreement the interest element will be 12/78ths of the total. In the second it will be 11/78ths, and so on.

The same principle can be used for any period of agreement. Equally the interest figures can include the finance company's profit calculated on the same basis if they so wish. Although it may sound complicated anyone with a pocket calculator should be able to master the technique in a few minutes!

Rule 163

A rule of the Stock Exchange, London, under which shares of some companies can be freely bought and sold without the company concerned having to meet all the strict requirements normally asked for. There are a number of types of shares covered by this rule. There are shares which are 'listed' on an overseas stock exchange whose rules are less demanding than those of London. There are shares in companies which do nothing but explore for minerals. These are often very risky and the companies concerned could not meet the normal requirement of showing a sound track record. There are also shares in 'private' companies (q.v.) in which there is obviously public interest and the need for a market. A good example of this type are the shares in football clubs.

The idea behind Rule 163 is to provide a market place for shares which a number of investors are likely to want to buy and sell. In effect the Stock Exchange provides the facility but, at the same time, says 'Watch out!'

S

Sales day book

A daily record of sales. In effect a list of all invoices and credit notes issued on a particular day. The day book provides the posting medium to sales accounts in double entry bookkeeping systems and totals for control accounts. It also gives a means of analysing sales by product group or region. This is usually done by allocating a code number to each invoice which indicates a particular category of product or other analysis heading. The day book shows both the total amount of the invoice and the coded analysis. At the end of the period all the analysis columns can be added up and agreed with the total sales made. This provides a useful check on the accuracy of the record as well as on management information.

Sales ledger

A record containing the accounts of transactions with individual customers. Usually organised alphabetically, sales ledger accounts show both sales made and cash received. The balance due to the business is usually shown in total but in some systems it is shown as the 'open items' for which cash has not been received. In many mechanised and some manual systems the sales ledger is replaced by unmatched invoices arranged alphabetically and conventional records are dispensed with. This is obviously more economical than keeping ledger accounts and the controls available on computers ensure that items do not get lost. It seems likely that in the next few years all sales accounting systems will change to this method.

Save As You Earn (S.A.Y.E.)

A commitment taken on by an employee of a company to save money through a company scheme for a period of at least five years leading to the purchase of company shares at an agreed price. This type of scheme provides the employee with an opportunity to buy a stake in his company through regular saving. The basis of some schemes is a share option arrangement (q.v.). The number and value of the options created by such schemes must be shown in the annual accounts of the company concerned.

Scrip issue

A free issue of shares to existing shareholders in a company. Basically the issue of 'scrip' is a bookkeeping transaction which gives the ordinary shareholder no more nor less than he is already entitled to. The idea of this sort of issue is to increase the *number* of shares held by using the reserves of the company to 'pay them up'. It works like this:

A company has the following capital:

	£'000
Ordinary shares of £1	120
Preference shares of £1	70
Reserves	450
Capital and reserves	640

The directors decide to give each ordinary shareholder a '1 for 1' scrip issue so each shareholder will get another £1 share, paid up, in addition to the one he holds already. The bookkeeping works like this:

	£'000	£'000
Ordinary shares of £1		120
Plus 'scrip' issue		120
		240
Preference shares		70
Reserves	450	
Less used to pay up 'scrip'	120	330
Capital and reserves		640

The effect of a scrip issue is to make more shares available for sale. However, the earnings per share are 'distributed' in exact proportion to the number of new shares created. Scrip issues are also referred to as 'bonus' or 'capitalisation' issues.

There is no tax payable on a scrip issue.

Self assessment

A system by which an 'individual' calculates his own tax liability and pays tax on this basis. It is not used for Income Tax or Corporation Tax in this country although it is common overseas, particularly in the United States. Such a system is based on the tax collecting authority trusting the taxpayer not to cheat, backed up by the tax authorities with a selective checking process. Understandably the penalties for failing to declare income correctly are more severe than in countries in which self-assessment is not used. Many people have advocated the use of this system in the U.K. and it would certainly reduce the administrative burden on the Inland Revenue. However, there are equally strong arguments for retaining the present system which has been established here for very many years.

Share option

A right to buy new shares in a company at a fixed price at some future date. Unlike warrants (q.v.) share options are not transferable and are usually granted to individuals who have some special relationship with a company. They are often given to directors or senior employees as a form of incentive. They may equally well be given to someone who makes a loan to a company. The existence of share options which are outstanding must be shown in the accounts of the company concerned. The right to an option is sometimes established by an initial payment being made by the prospective shareholder (for example, 1p in the pound of nominal value), the balance being paid when the option is exercised. The right to an option is also commonly lost if the special relationship ends. Thus a director with a share option entitlement may have to give it up if he leaves the company.

Share premium

An amount paid on the issue of shares in a company above the face value of the shares. For example, a company may decide to issue some new £1 ordinary shares. The company's record and assets might justify an asking price of £2 per share. When the new shareholders pay the £2 for the share, £1 will be allocated to the share capital account and £1 to the share premium account. For all intents and purposes share premiums are treated in the accounts in the same way as equity capital (q.v.). Once paid, share premium cannot be distributed to shareholders, or the total amount reduced, without the permission of the courts.

Sinking fund

A sum of money set aside, year by year, to pay off a known future commitment. If a company has to repay a loan of £100,000 in ten years' time, it may set up a sinking fund, and pay in £10,000 a year to make sure it has sufficient cash available when the payment is due. Strictly such a fund should be kept separate from other company money and, perhaps, invested in safe securities. Few companies nowadays adopt this method because it ties up capital that can be better used in the business. They may prefer to provide for the future payment by writing off a certain amount each year against profits, or simply live in the hope that they will either have enough cash available at the right time or that they can replace the sum due by borrowing from someone else.

Sources and applications of funds

A statement showing how a business has earned or acquired funds in a period and how they have been spent. Sources and applications of funds statements are different from cash flow (q.v.) since they show all investments of funds on the profit and loss account and balance sheet, and not just changes in the level of cash at the bank.

The form that these statements should take when included in sets of accounts is laid down by the Institute of Chartered Accountants. Basically the format is as follows:

	£	£
Profit per the profit and loss account		X
Add: Depreciation charged in the accounts		X
		X
Add: Proceeds of sales of assets, funds raised from shareholders etc.		X
		X
Changes in working capital		
Funds received from increased creditors or reduced debtors	X	
Less: Funds applied to reducing creditors or increasing debtors	X	
Net change in working capital		X
		X
Less: Funds spent on acquiring fixed assets		X
Net change in funds reflected in bank balances		X

The sources and applications of funds statement gives a very good idea of whether the firm is proving able to finance its own business without increasing its borrowings from other sources. If it constantly fails to live on its own resources the statement can give an early warning of impending problems.

S.S.A.P.

The abbreviations of 'Statement of Standard Accounting Principle' which is a rule to be applied by members of the Institute of Chartered Accountants in accounts prepared or audited by them. S.S.A.P.s have been issued since the early 1970s on a variety of accounting topics. They are intended to ensure that all company accounts are prepared on a consistent basis. Some have been accepted with little enthusiasm by commerce and industry and an increasing number of accounts are qualified for non-compliance with them. They are issued after a period of consultation with both those who prepare and those who use accounts. They have made an undoubted contribution to bringing accounts into a more regular structure.

Stag

A person who applies for new issue of shares expecting to sell at a profit when they are first bought and sold on the Stock Exchange. Many new issues of shares are over-subscribed, for example, if a million shares are offered to the public, applications might be made for two million or even five million shares. The issuing house 'rations' the shares among those applying. If the offer is attractive those who do not get all the shares they applied for often buy shares in the market when dealing starts, a week or two after the issue. This can create a 'premium' by pushing up the share price, which makes it attractive for the 'stag' to sell those allotted to him. If, of course, the over-subscription is caused wholly by 'stagging' there may be no premium at all and the stag may have to sell at a loss. Although stagging may seem to be simply gambling it actually performs a useful function in making an active market for new shares. The issuing-house can also use the stag's application money for a few days which can make a useful contribution to reducing the costs of the issue.

Stamp duties

Levies payable to the government calculated as a percentage of the value of issues of new capital in companies, sales of securities and other transfers of assets. Many regard stamp duties as something of an anachronism, clung to more through sentiment than their revenue-raising potential. However, every transfer of shares (except British Government Securities) carries a levy of 2% and every contribution to the capital of a company one of 1%. The sums involved can therefore be quite significant. Stamp duty, like most taxes, is subject to complicated law which needs an expert to unravel. This law provides relief for company reconstructions and mergers. Stamp duty reform will doubtless form part of E.E.C. harmonisation and it seems probable the whole complex structure will be changed, if not simplified, in the next ten to fifteen years.

Standard cost

A figure used to help fix prices and control costs. It is normally calculated by measuring how much material and labour is needed to make an item of production. These amounts are valued at fixed prices and part of the firm's overhead costs is allocated to each item:

	£
2 metres of metal at £1 per metre	2.00
½ hr direct labour at £2 per hour	1.00
Direct costs	3.00
Overheads (200% of direct costs)	6.00
	9.00 = standard cost

By adding a profit margin to this figure a selling price can be arrived at. Efficiency can be measured by comparing actual costs incurred in producing and selling the item.

In practice many firms tend to rely on previous experience to arrive at standard costs, rather than on the more expensive methods of detailed measurement. By so doing they run the risk of failing to allow for inflation and the effects of new technology.

Stock

A term with two meanings in common financial use. Firstly it describes the value of materials and finished goods shown on a balance sheet. Stock, or 'stock in trade', has to be counted and valued at each balance sheet date. This is because the amount of money involved cannot be accurately measured in the accounting records, even if a costing system is in use. Stocktaking is, in consequence, an important annual event in which the company's auditors take a close interest.

Many companies keep a regular check on stock levels by using 'perpetual inventory' checking techniques (q.v.). This gives management a way of testing the accuracy of recording systems and, at the same time, finding out whether or not goods are being wasted or stolen. In North America the term 'inventory' is used instead of stock.

In many accounts stock and work in progress values are shown as one total. This usually makes little difference to the reader of the accounts.

The second use of the word 'stock' is as a description for a loan made to a company on fixed terms. Loan stocks can be of many types involving different rights to interest and capital repayment. The familiar phrase 'stocks and shares' is meant to embrace loan stocks in their various forms as well as ordinary and other types of shares.

Stock relief

An allowance given as a concession by the government, which permits traders to reduce the amount of their tax bill by a proportion of the increase in the value of their stocks in a year. It was first given in 1975 because traders faced with the problem of financing increasing stocks during a period of rapid inflation could not find the cash to do this and also pay their tax bills. The concession originally only allowed the tax to be 'deferred' and did not therefore reduce the bill for good. The stock relief given to traders therefore constituted a large part of the 'deferred tax' (q.v.) shown on balance sheets. In recent years it has been recognised that much of this tax will never be recovered in practice. As a result a scheme of progressively forgiving traders this liability was introduced in 1978.

The amount of the relief is based on a formula that is best left, in practice, to taxation specialists to interpret.

Sum of the digits

A method for calculating how much should be charged in the profit and loss account for the wear and tear on assets based on adding together the number of years of their useful working life. The calculation is made in exactly the same way as that used for interest spreading under the rule of 78 (q.v.). The sum of the digits is rarely used in the United Kingdom although it is occasionally found in leasing companies. It is particularly useful when there is a heavy investment in the early years of a project when the depreciation charge needs to be correspondingly high.

Sur Tax

A tax on high levels of income which was abandoned in 1973. Sur Tax and its predecessor, Super Tax, were administered separately from the Income Tax system and it was often argued that the yield from the tax did little more than pay for its operation. Sur Tax was replaced by higher rates of tax forming an integral part of the Income Tax structure. This is clearly much simpler to administer and it seems unlikely that Sur Tax will ever be re-introduced.

T

Tax avoidance

The process of taking steps to minimise the tax bill of an individual or a company. Tax avoidance is a legitimate activity which must not be confused with tax evasion (q.v.), which is illegal. Tax avoidance schemes become increasingly interesting to tax payers as tax rates rise. They are sometimes dicussed in detail with the Inland Revenue before they are implemented. The reason why this can be done in the U.K. is that the tax system relies on the interpretation of statute and if a clever accountant or lawyer can find a 'loophole' in the wording there is nothing that the Inland Revenue can do about it. At least that is the position until a new Finance Act closes the loophole!

Tax credit

A credit taken by one tax payer for tax paid on his behalf by another person or organisation. The most common example of a tax credit is the tax paid by a company on dividends before they are paid to its shareholders. Under Advanced Corporation Tax (A.C.T.) arrangements (q.v.), the shareholder gets a 'tax credit' on the amount actually paid. When the shareholder puts in his tax return he shows the amount received plus the tax credit. When the Tax Inspector assesses the shareholder's tax bill he knows that the tax represented by the tax credit has already been paid by the company, at the basic Income Tax Rate. If the shareholder's personal tax rate is higher than the basic rate the Inspector has only to claim the difference.

Tax evasion

The illegal misrepresentation of an individual's or a company's financial affairs made to evade the payment of tax. Most commonly tax evasion takes the form of failing to tell the Inland

Revenue the true amount of earnings in a period. However, there are many more complex forms of evasion engineered by unscrupulous individuals and company directors. The Enquiry Branch of the Inland Revenue has power to pursue tax evaders by enquiring into their affairs over a number of years. Severe penalties in terms of payments of tax undeclared, fines and imprisonment can be applied on prosecution.

Transfer price

The price at which goods or services are charged between departments within an organisation or between companies in a group. By definition a transfer price is different from the price which would be charged in the open market. It is often used to set a level of return to the charging department or company which reflects the cost incurred but not to include any element of profit. For example a car-manufacturing company may have a factory making body panels. These are shipped to an assembly plant which brings all the components together into the final product. If the panels were sold to the assembly unit at a price including profit it would be difficult for the company to keep track of the overall profit made on the sale of each vehicle. What is done is to fix a transfer price including sufficient overheads to allow the body panel factory to cover costs and make no profit or loss in a normal period. This has the obvious advantage of allowing the company to keep all profits in one place. It can also be used as a means of organising a company's tax affairs if it trades in more than one country.

Treasurer

The chief financial officer of a business using a North American form of organisation structure. The nearest U.K. equivalent to the Treasurer is the financial director. In practice the Treasurer has wider executive powers than his opposite number on this side of the Atlantic. He (or she) is also more likely to be a lawyer or banker than a qualified accountant, which is virtually a prerequisite for a financial director. The Treasurer's job gives a lot of emphasis to how money is raised and used within the business. Routine financial management rests with the controller (sometimes quaintly called comptroller) so the Treasurer can concentrate on broad financial policy. Many people feel that this clear separation of functions has made a significant contribution to the financial success of many American companies.

Treasury bills

A short term investment offered by the government to raise money to cover 'leads and lags' in its spending. They are issued each week by the Bank of England to anyone who would like to buy them. They have a face value of £100 although you cannot buy less than £5,000-worth at a time. The total amount of bills offered each week varies and they are effectively put up for auction to the highest bidder. The idea is that the government will pay the holder the full £100 in three months' time. They expect to have bids of less than £100 now. If for example, buyers bid £95 now, in three months' time they will make a capital £5 profit for each £100-worth bought. The difference between the bid price and £100 varies according to interest rate levels, market confidence and so on. There is always a reserve price and if the issue does not attract enough money, any unsold Bills are taken up by discount houses (q.v.).

Trial balance

A listing of all the balances on the books of a business at a particular date to prove that the entries, in total, have been made accurately. A trial balance is so called because several 'tries' are often needed before the books balance. The trial balance is a critical stage in proving the accuracy of a double entry book-keeping system before accounts are prepared. In it are incorporated the total debit balances and the total credit balances taken from the personal ledgers, the impersonal ledgers and the cash book.

A trial balance is normally used as a basic working document in the preparation of accounts. It is 'extended' by including, using double entry principles, debts due and owed not recorded in the system and adjustments between accounts. This extended form of the trial balance enables the accountant to prepare the profit and loss account and balance sheet directly from the balances on the ledger. It means that there is both a firm base to work from and also a means of checking that adjustments are made equally to debits and credits.

U

Underwriter

A person who makes a business out of taking over other people's risks for a fee. Most commonly an underwriter is a member of a group or 'syndicate' in the Lloyd's insurance market in London. These individuals stake their personal wealth on taking part of an insurance risk associated with fire, theft or other disaster in return for a portion of the premium charged to the insured person or company. In simple terms the underwriter assesses the extent of the risk, based on previous experience. He then decides how much premium should be paid to cover the risk and how much of the total he, and the fellow members of his syndicate, should bear. In almost every case a large risk is covered by a series of syndicates, each sharing in a part of the premium in porportion to their part of the risk. Using skill and judgement they balance income and losses (from claims) and end up making a profit.

Other risks not connected with insurance are underwritten by financial institutions. For example, the risk that shares offered to the public will not be bought will be underwritten by a merchant bank, stockbroker, a pension fund and so on. Once again a fee is charged to the person who would otherwise carry the risk himself.

Undischarged bankrupt

A person who has been made bankrupt but who has not been 'discharged' by the court and absolved from any remaining liabilities. By becoming officially bankrupt a person recognises that he can no longer manage his financial affairs himself and settle his debts. Bankruptcy involves handing over this responsibility to an officer of the court, the Official Receiver or some other suitable person as trustee. It is a painful business. It involves drawing up a complete account of everything that the person has and owes. He or she must appear in public to explain how they got into such a mess and how they propose to get out of it. After this the court will completely manage the person's finances paying over whatever can be spared, from the person's income after their court expenses have been paid, to creditors. The undischarged bankrupt cannot take credit or become a director of a company without the permission of the court.

If the bankupt can pay off all his debts over a period he can go to the court and expect to be discharged. Even if this is not in prospect he can still ask to be discharged on the basis that he has 'served his sentence' and wants to make a clean start. The court will then use its discretion either to discharge him or not.

Unlimited company

A company in which the shareholders accept unlimited liability for its debts. Such companies do not use the word 'Limited' in their titles, for obvious reasons! The unlimited company is in many respects equivalent to a partnership. The basic similarity is that partners share unlimited responsibility for trading debts. In the case of an unlimited liability company the shareholders share this liability in proportion to the shares they own. In virtually every other respect an unlimited liability company is organised and run like any other company. The directors are excused, however, from filing their annual accounts with the Registrar of Companies. The unlimited liability company is not a common species. It is most often used as a vehicle for professional services where the advantages of having shares to buy and sell are combined with acceptance of an open-ended personal liability.

Unquoted share

Any share in a company which cannot be bought and sold on a stock exchange. This applies to the vast majority of shares since most companies are 'private' as opposed to 'public'. Since there is no public market for such shares their value cannot be ascertained by looking at *The Financial Times* or the Stock Exchange List. Nor can they be turned into cash unless there is a particular buyer willing to take them and risk the same difficulty of future disposal. Of course if a public company absorbs a private company by buying its shares this difficulty is overcome since the value of the unquoted shares thereafter forms part of the value of the quoted shares of the buyer. However, any buyer of unquoted shares is likely to strike a harder bargain than if he was buying the quoted equivalent.

The main advantage of shares being unquoted is that the company does not have to comply with many and stringent rules applied by the Stock Exchange to shares bought and sold on the open market. The main disadvantage is that they are inevitably worth less than the quoted equivalents for the very reason that they are more difficult to sell.

V

Value Added Tax (V.A.T.)

A tax on goods and services, calculated as a percentage of the price paid by the customer, collected in stages through the process of production and sale. The V.A.T. system employs an unusual principle of calculating liability. Firstly a trader must be 'registered' and to be so must show sales of at least £13,500 a year. When the trader buys goods the V.A.T. included in the buying price is totalled up. This is known as his 'input' V.A.T. When he sells goods the trader adds V.A.T. at the appropriate rate to the selling price. The total V.A.T. the trader charges to his customers in a period is called 'output V.A.T.'. When assessing the V.A.T. the trader owes in a period, the 'input' total is deducted from the 'output' total. In simple terms a V.A.T. calculation might be:

	Goods £	*V.A.T. @15%* £	*TOTAL* £
Sales in the period	200	30	230
Purchases in the period	(100)	(15)	(115)
Difference	100	15	115

As can be seen, when the V.A.T. due (£15) is paid, the trader's profit is the same as if there had been no V.A.T, (£100). The trader does not *bear* the tax, he simply collects it. The burden of V.A.T. falls on the consumer. The complications of the V.A.T. system include exemptions from the scheme and zero-rated articles. The Customs & Excise publish extensive and simple guides to V.A.T. administration.

Variance

The amount of the difference between an actual amount and an estimate of that amount made earlier. Most commonly variances crop up in costing and management accounting. The term 'variance' may be used at the top of a column of figures showing differences between budget and actual results in a period. Finding explanations for these differences is often called 'variance analysis'. In costing systems the term is used to describe differences arising from a particular cause, for example, volume variance, price variance, efficiency variance and calendar variance. Each of these is separately defined elsewhere.

The importance of management knowing why variances in financial results have occurred lies in the insight they can give into both efficiency and forecasting skill. The variance can thus tell you that you have done something better or worse than you should have done. Or it can tell you that you under- or over-estimated what it would really cost to do something, even at maximum efficiency. Usually it tells you something of each and a manager's job is to decide what action he must take to eliminate variances in future.

Venture capital

Money put into a new enterprise which may all be lost if it fails. Usually venture capital is in the form of ordinary shares or an unsecured loan. The individual or institution providing the funds recognises the gamble inherent in the new enterprise by being prepared to lose all his money if it fails. If it succeeds, of course, he hopes to make a large profit on the investment. A number of merchant banks offer venture capital funds for smaller businesses. Usually they expect to be in a position to control the use of the money they put in and often put a director on the board of the company. Traditionally new ventures have usually been launched by established businesses who can afford to stand at least a part of any potential loss. Venture capital may be raised by such companies from a much wider range of sources than those available to the smaller business. These include institutions such as insurance companies, pension funds and the Stock Market itself. In practice probably the largest providers of venture capital, albeit in small individual sums, are the high street banks. They regularly support the 'one-man businesses' with loans with little security. In all these cases it is not only the 'venture' itself but the capabilities of the person proposing it which are the most important factors.

Volume variance

The financial effect on the recovery of overheads in an accounting period of making fewer or more of a product than predicted. Essentially an analytical tool of costing, the volume variance shows the manager the effect on the cost of each unit made and on profits of being more or less busy in production than expected. The effect is caused by the fact that fixed overheads (q.v.) have to be recovered by sharing them out over all items made. Management must decide how much overhead each item will attract when fixing prices before they are made. This must be based on an estimate of how many will be made. If fewer are actually made than expected each item will have to carry more overhead than expected and vice versa. This example shows simply how it works:

	Estimate	*More Made*	*Fewer Made*
Number of items	10,000	12,000	8,000
Overheads	£30,000	£30,000	£30,000
Overhead cost per item	£3	£2.50	£3.75
Volume Variance (per item)	—	− 50p	+ 75p
Volume Variance based on original estimate	—	12,000 × 50p = £6,000 saving	8,000 × 75p = £6,000 less

If the price is fixed on the basis of the £3 overhead cost the volume variance will mean either £6,000 more profit (12,000 made) or £6,000 less profit (8,000 made).

W

Warrant

A right given by a company to someone to buy new shares at a fixed price (the exercise price). Warrants are usually issued as part of a 'package' including unsecured loan stock. The idea is that more people are likely to put money into a company as unsecured loans if there is a 'sweetener'. The warrants, by granting the holder the chance to buy equity in the future, provide the incentive needed. Obviously the exercise price involves a gamble depending whether you think the share price will rise or fall. The warrants are often bought and sold before the 'exercise period', the period of weeks or months when the equity shares can be bought at the exercise price. If for example the warrants carry a right to buy shares at 250p in two years' time they will be more valuable if the shares are now worth 300p than if they are worth 150p. As the exercise period approaches the speculative element diminishes and ultimately the warrant becomes worthless at its end.

Work in progress

The value of goods still in the process of manufacture which is included amongst current assets on the balance sheet. The term is applied widely in many types of organisations. It can cover conventional physical products being made in a factory or, equally, for example, the time spent to a particular date by the staff of an advertising agency on a client account. The general principles of the calculation of value are, however, the same. These are that the total should include:

The costs of materials *specifically* allocated or used to date.
The costs of labour or machine time *specifically* spent to date.
An *allocation* of overheads related to either one or both of the above items.

It is usually the last of those principles which creates the most difficulty in practice in assessing the total value of work in progress. Endless hours of highly experienced accountants' time are spent around the end of companies' financial years tussling with it. A further complication is the question of whether or not an element of profit should be included in work in progress value. The usual approach is to make sure that the valuation is conservative.